Beyond Nice

149 Ideas to Nurture Kindness in Young Children

by
Stuart Stotts

BIG VALLEY PRESS

© Big Valley Press 2015

Big Valley Press
401 E Holum St.
Deforest, Wi. 53532
www.BigValleyPress.com

ISBN-987-0-9765372-1-2

Library of Congress Control Number: 2015904136

Stotts, Stuart 1957-

Beyond Nice: 149 Ideas to Nurture Kindness in Young Children/Stuart Stotts

Summary: Ideas, activities, and reflections to encourage kindness in young children

BIG VALLEY PRESS

Dedicated to my friend Charlie Knower
for his kindness
and for our conversations when
seeds for this book began to bloom.

Be kind whenever possible.
It is always possible.
The Dalai Lama

CONTENTS

INTRODUCTION

Three things in human life are important:
the first is to be kind; the second is to be kind;
and the third is to be kind.

Henry James

When I walk into an early childhood classroom the first thing I look for is the carpet. It's easy to find. It's probably in a corner, and there's often a large calendar on the wall, a bookshelf on one side, and a comfortable, strategically placed, adult-sized chair.

The carpet, sometimes also referred to as the rug, is where kids and teachers meet. It's a gathering place filled with songs, chants, and stories. It's where I want to be.

As I head toward the carpet, I make my way through kids who are scattered around the room. Some are drawing, some are busy at a kitchen or workbench, and some are building with blocks or looking at books. They're curious about me, and they ask about my guitar case. Sometimes I say it's a piano, and they laugh and become instantly more curious. I tell them my name is Stuart and I've come to sing with them.

Over twenty-five years ago I entered just such a classroom in Sun Prairie, Wisconsin. Children gathered around me as I unpacked my guitar.

A four-year old boy named Tim suddenly burst into tears. "I don't want to sing," he wailed.

His teacher looked horrified and embarrassed and I could tell that she wanted to chastise him. I took a deep breath and smiled at Tim. "You don't have to sing if you don't want to."

Tim looked shocked and then grateful. Another student put her arm around him, and he relaxed. I began a song. Soon all of us, including Tim, were singing together.

By my next visit to the classroom, Tim was my best buddy.

That moment was one of many in my thirty years of singing with children that revealed lessons about the power of kindness and empathy.

Over the last few years, I've become particularly interested in how kindness is taught to young children. I know that teachers want their students to be kind. Parents want the same thing. We all struggle to do the right thing by our children, and yet we often don't know what to do.

I believe that kindness is our most important human attribute. I also believe we all have the capacity for kindness, that it can be taught, or at least nurtured, and that we need to be wide and creative in our approaches to how we do that teaching and nurturing.

The earlier we start, the better. When children are raised in kind families they receive a strong foundation. But lots of kids aren't raised that way, and even if they are, every child benefits from focusing on kindness. As Frederick Douglass said, "It's easier to build strong children than to repair broken men."

Brain science demonstrates that a person's ability to attach and connect with others is largely set in the first five years. Early childhood is the time for children to learn how it feels to give and receive kindness. They can carry that feeling and orientation for the rest of their lives. We should put our best resources toward educating young children, and that includes focusing on nurturing connection, relationships, and kindness.

K I N D N E S S & S C I E N C E

In 1991, 900 at-risk children around the country were chosen to participate in a study. Half of the children received intensive teaching in social-emotional intelligence, and half did not. By age 25, those who were enrolled in the special program not only had done better in school, but they also had lower rates of arrests and fewer mental health and substance abuse issues. The American Journal of Psychiatry published the results of this study in September 2014.

Classrooms, like terrariums, are microcosms of the world. I've seen kids tattle, hit, grab, and cry. I've also seen them share, comfort, listen, and laugh. If our classrooms, and our families, are like terrariums, then we need to make them incubators of compassion, hotbeds of kindness, and envelopes of empathy.

I often get the sense that it has become more difficult to nurture kindness than it used to be, and that kindness itself is on the wane. Many families are under tremendous stress, feeling pressed for time and facing economic hardship. In addition, teachers often feel so much pressure to attend to academics that they don't focus on social learning. Children's greater exposure to electronics seems to have further detrimental impacts on social skills, making the task of nurturing kindness even more important.

We mostly teach kindness through verbal avenues. We talk with children. We lecture them. We intervene and have kids reflect on their actions. We ask them to repeat affirmations of kindness or use specific language that reflects our idea of what kindness is or how someone should feel.

This approach isn't enough to reach the deeper levels that need to be accessed if we are to move toward a kinder posture. The attitudes and feelings around kindness reach into places beyond words, shaping our actions through unconscious waves and invisible currents. If we want to influence kindness, we have to move beyond talking and into action, through arts, movement, reflection, tone of voice, and habits.

As childcare expert Ruth Wilson writes, "We know that children don't learn to care by talking about what it means to care or listening to others talking about care. To learn to care, children need to experience being cared for, see others engaged in the act of caring, and participate in meaningful activities where they nurture and care for something outside of themselves."

We can weave kindness into every lesson and interaction. Kindness isn't a separate unit like colors or days of the week. Explicit instruction, exploration, and reflection throughout the year expand the awareness and practice of kindness.

This book is the result of conversations with teachers and parents as well as my own observations and interactions. I've been more of a collector than a creator, and I'm grateful to everyone who shared ideas with me.

Spreading kindness can seem like a very simple and a very large task, all at the same time. I've been fortunate to receive tremendous kindness in my life. Noticing or experiencing kindness nudges me in the direction of being kinder myself. I think this is how kindness shapes the world—in everyday, ordinary, warm interactions with the people around us. I know we can make a difference in children's lives by focusing on kindness. Ultimately, the difference we make will spread out into the world, making life richer and sweeter for all of us.

HOW TO USE THIS BOOK

People learn best when they take charge of how they learn rather than passively accepting what's handed to them. I agree with Isaac Asimov when he says, "Self-education is, I firmly believe, the only kind of education there is."

That should apply to how you use this book.

This book is most appropriate for teachers and parents of children between the ages of 3 and 8. Some strategies will work with children younger than that, and some can even be used with adults. You will have to gauge which ones will be most effective for the children you know.

Social and emotional development is central to early childhood education. A range of approaches to exploring kindness will stretch your own comfort zone and reach a variety of children's learning styles and personalities. For these reasons, I've gathered activities that allow children to experience, feel, move, create, and sing, as well as talk and listen.

You may choose to start with activities or themes that fit a particular interest or need of yours, or you may want to proceed in order through the chapters. Activities form the bulk of this book, and you will find more general information at the back.

The resources listed offer places to look for greater depth on many related subjects, including research, standards, learning approaches, and history. Every chapter has relevant web links, and you can access them at **www.stuartstotts.com/kindness-resources/**.

Teachers will find activities for large and small groups, as well as for individuals. Many of these activities fit within the context of other units of learning that take place during the year. Some of these ideas focus on teaching and exploring kindness through activity and reflection. Some focus more on creating kindness through environment and collaboration.

Parents can explore activities or ideas with their own children, or perhaps in short sessions with a small group of friends. Some of these strategies might encourage conversations at dinner or in the car. In addition, having a shared concept and vocabulary around kindness may help families as they seek to instill positive values in their children.

Have fun doing these activities! Kindness is a serious subject, but it doesn't have to be heavy or difficult. The emotional atmosphere may be more important than any lesson taught. The goal is for children to experience positive feelings and align themselves with wanting to give and receive more kindness.

Kindness is a practice, which means it's both an ongoing way of being and a goal that is achieved through repetition. We don't ever finally arrive at kindness, but we head in that direction and find our way through individual routes, twisting and turning, getting off track sometimes and getting lost. Find your own way through this book, and come back to it when you need further ideas or inspiration.

WHAT IS KINDNESS? AND WHY DOES IT MATTER?

A man's true delight is to do
the things he was made for.
He was made to show goodwill
toward his kind.

Marcus Aurelius

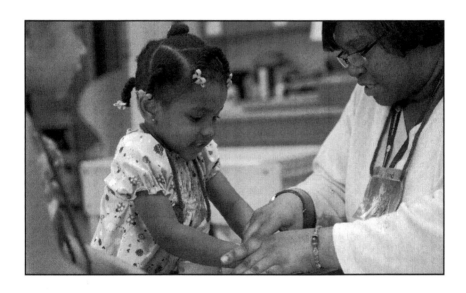

AN OLD CHEROKEE man was talking to his grandson. "A fight is going on inside me," he said to the boy. The boy's eyes widened with apprehension.

The old man went on. "It's a vicious fight between two wolves. One is evil—filled with anger, envy, arrogance, lies, false pride, and ego."

The boy nodded, picturing and fearing the image of the evil wolf.

The old man continued. "The other wolf is good—filled with joy, peace, love, humility, empathy, generosity, and compassion. The same fight is going on inside you—and inside every other person, too."

The boy thought for a minute, imagining the violent battle between the two wild animals. Finally he asked his grandfather, "Which wolf will win in you, grandfather?"

The old man replied, "The one I feed."

The wise man in the story may say that the winner of the battle inside himself will depend on which wolf he chooses to feed, but young children don't feed themselves. They depend on us.

We can argue about whether people are inherently good or bad by nature, but I believe that we have both capacities within us. There is considerable research showing that we are hardwired for compassion, even though human history might suggest otherwise.

Think of someone who embodies kindness to you. Who do you know in your life, or from reputation or public image, that comes to mind when you hear the word kindness?

Imagine sitting down for a quiet conversation with that person. What qualities would stand out? You might use words like: gentle, caring, compassionate, patient, selfless, generous, focused, present, loving, listening.

If we define kindness by synonym, any of those words add to the picture we want to create. Like darts thrown at a dartboard, these descriptors all approach the target, the bull's-eye, the heart of kindness. Kindness is an umbrella for any number of related concepts: generosity, forgiveness, gratitude, empathy, courtesy, and respect.

The Oxford dictionary defines kindness as, "Noun; the quality of being friendly, generous, and considerate."

The authors of the book *On Kindness* say that the kind life is "a life lived in instinctive identification with the vulnerabilities and attractions of others."

There are many other good definitions. Here's mine: **Kindness is the active inclination to do well for or think well of others without expectation of return.**

Language Origins

The root of the word "kindness" is derived from gecynde, or gakundi, found in Middle English writing as early as 900 C.E. Some of the original meanings include: property, family, birth, character, and even cow. All of these original meanings had something to do with ideas of origin and belonging.

One strand of the word's roots can be found in its relation to the word "kin" or "kindred," connecting to the concept of natural characteristics. When I ask, "What kind of person is he?" I'm trying to understand, "Who is he at heart?"

Kindness also does come from the word for cow, which might explain the expression "the milk of human kindness." However, kindness also seems to imply relatedness, belonging, nurture, and family. This root leads to questions like: "Do I belong with this person?" "Are we part of the same family?" "How do we relate?"

Relatedness is the heart of kindness. Teaching kindness is about expanding the circle of relationship and belonging. When we are connected in a positive way, kindness is the natural response.

Moral Virtue

Kindness can be seen as a moral virtue. Being kind is the right thing to do. Religions preach kindness, and teachers and parents admonish children in its direction. "Be a good person" and "be kind" have become synonymous. While it's true that kindness makes for a good ethical foundation, kindness is more than just a set of rules to follow.

In *The Moral Life of Children* author Robert Coles writes, "It is a mistake to think of morality as a set of external standards that adults foist upon an unknowing or unwilling child." Instead, we can expect that children will develop their own sense of morality—including kindness—through role modeling, experience, dialogue, and encouragement.

Developmental View

My parents were from the South, and being nice, sometimes also called "making nice," was an essential component of being civilized. I learned to be nice, which meant being polite and including everyone in the conversation or activity. It meant presenting a positive face to the world and being easy and acceptable to those around me. Being nice makes life smoother.

My parents were both very nice people, but I was fortunate that they were also kind. The distinction matters.

Being nice doesn't always mean being kind. If nice is about the outer face, manners, and style, kindness is about a deeper impulse to treat people well and to look for good.

We want kids to be nice to each other and to everyone. But we don't want them to stop there; we want them to be kind, too. **Kindness reaches into the heart of what it means to be human.**

Learning kindness proceeds in two phases. In the first stage children learn to be kind because it makes others happy. Children learn that tantrums, selfishness, and rude behavior don't get them far with their parents, teachers, or even their friends, so they moderate their ego impulses.

Most children are fairly successful at this. They learn what kinds of actions are acceptable, and they get with the program, most of the time. When they're stressed, tired, or in unpleasant situations, they act out or lose self-control. But for most kids, that's the exception, not the norm.

In this phase of learning, children become socialized to kindness because it makes life easier. Adults around them reinforce this kind of behavior. However, I would call this more nice than kind, because these behaviors and outward actions may or may not reflect the true feelings inside.

Deep kindness, the second phase, is based less on reaction to the world and more on internal orientation. This type of kindness occurs regardless of one's situation or relationship to the other. It's not just about smoothing over social interactions. As the French essayist Joseph Joubert says, "A part of kindness consists of loving people more than they deserve."

This kind of kindness requires empathy and fellow feeling, regardless of the circumstance. It's about turning the other cheek. While we can lay a foundation for it in early childhood, deep kindness is the work of a lifetime. However, without the foundation, it's very difficult to cultivate later.

Kindness in this respect is a psychological virtue. Martin Luther King said, "I have decided to stick with love. Hatred is too great a burden to bear." What King is intimating here is that being unkind hurts the one who demonstrates the feeling. A friend of mine once said resentment is like "drinking poison and hoping the other person dies."

I think of myself as a kind person, and I think others would describe me that way. Nevertheless, working on this book has reminded me of the times and ways I've acted unkindly. I can't think of one act of unkindness that I'm proud of. Sometimes the evil wolf wins.

Ultimately, kindness feels good. It packs a psychological payoff. Instead of hoping to instill kindness through preaching or lecturing, we can allow and encourage children to feel the warmth of kindness in themselves and to experience and notice the inner glow that accompanies it.

KINDNESS & SCIENCE

Patricia O'Grady, a neuroscientist at the University of Tampa, examines how kindness affects the brain. Dr. O'Grady says, "Kindness changes the brain by the experience of kindness. Children and adolescents do not learn kindness by only thinking about it and talking about it. Kindness is best learned by feeling it so that they can reproduce it."

We don't need to make kids be kind. And we couldn't, anyway. We need to give them opportunities, encourage them, and ultimately let them discover kindness and the good feelings that accompany it. Then we need to help them become aware of and find the words to express how they feel when they experience kindness—and also when they don't.

Choosing to Be Kind

We're nice because it helps us to get along. But when we choose to be kind, even in the face of difficulty, hostility, and bad history, kindness trumps grudges and grumpiness and changes our world and ourselves.

Kindness matters to the health of the world. The quality of our daily interactions, the way we care for the less fortunate, the feeling within our families, and the atmosphere in schools and workplaces are all sweetened by consistent kindness. It's only in the imaginations of warriors, criminals, demagogues, and profiteers that kindness is denigrated, misnamed as weakness or ungrounded optimism.

Kindness makes day-to-day life better.

K I N D N E S S & S C I E N C E

Recent research supports the idea that kindness boosts happiness.

Studies suggest that the positive benefits we receive from kindness include mental and physical benefits. Not only does it feel better to be kind, it may help you to live longer and be healthier. Other research studies have shown correlations between happiness and generous behavior, suggesting that if you want to increase happiness, increase kindness, and vice versa.

There is no research that indicates that humans are fundamentally competitive or that ruthlessness is "just human nature." We are what we are raised to be. We become the wolf we feed.

The "good" and the "bad," the light and the dark, the kind and the unkind live side by side in each of us, balanced daily on a scale that tilts from side to side. Martin Luther King said that the moral arc of the universe tends toward justice. I would say the same—most days, the arc of the universe leans toward kindness.

We want children to learn and experience for themselves that becoming their "best selves" includes a concern for the larger community. Children move from kindness as a set of rules to kindness as an expression of who they are. This is not a duty; rather, it's how we express and feel the best part of being human.

WHAT NOT TO DO

First, do no harm.

The Hippocratic Oath

THERE ARE SOME things to avoid in teaching kindness, and while they may seem obvious, I've made mistakes along these lines, as have many teachers I've talked with. It's worthwhile to name what to avoid.

The first is **shaming**. Shaming is never a good thing. That doesn't mean we shouldn't regret what we've done—that's guilt. The difference is that shame is felt as a reflection of who we are, which is damaging in the long run. It's the difference between, "I'm angry because you lied to me" and "I'm angry because you're a liar." A long-term sense of shame creates low self-esteem and relationship problems in many different environments. Focusing on the behavior rather than on the person is a straightforward guideline for any intervention, whether positive or negative.

Lecturing doesn't work. Watch a kid's eyes when you're lecturing. If you are being harsh or forceful, you'll see their eyes open wide, reflecting fear. Soon enough, though, their expression turns to boredom. Short sentences or statements are enough. Lecturing doesn't work very often in any situation, but with young children, the point you are trying to make shouldn't take more than about twenty seconds. After that, no matter how eloquently or articulately you are speaking, you've already lost your audience. Lecturing might feel good to those who deliver the lecture, but that doesn't mean a lecture teaches effectively.

Rewards detract from intrinsic motivation. Kids can learn about kindness without receiving stickers or candy for perceived "good" actions. The work of Alfie Kohn perhaps best addresses the problems with these kinds of interventions. We shouldn't need to be rewarded for doing the right thing; in fact, when we are rewarded, we are less likely to repeat a kind action without being rewarded. The old aphorism "kindness is its own reward," says it simply and best.

Praise or positive feedback should focus on your own reaction and a child's actions without ascribing qualities to that child. Children take a great deal of their self-image from adults, and we need to be careful to expand their inner lives as well. To say, "I felt really good when I saw you share your candy," has a different orientation from, "You are such a good boy for sharing." Others would go further and keep their own reactions out of it, saying simply, "Thank you for sharing your candy" or, "That was a kind decision." We don't want to raise kids to be people pleasers, but when they are young, they do need direct guidance and reinforcement. Noticing and naming what you see gives them the chance to internalize their response and understanding rather than depending on an adult to create the framework.

While teachers may want to **focus** on kindness, the concept shouldn't be relegated to a "kindness week," possibly followed by an "honesty week" or "respect week." Kindness should be woven into everyday activities throughout the year, not dealt with as a concept to be covered before moving on.

Last of all, two internal attitudes. **Don't blame** yourself for what isn't working, and **don't give up**. Sometimes teaching kindness is difficult. The path toward kindness is worth traveling, but sometimes it's uphill. In the face of failure—or success— keep going. The journey is rich and worthwhile.

ROLE MODELING

What parents teach is themselves, as models of what is human—by their moods, their reactions, their facial expressions and actions. These are the real things parents need to be aware of.

Magda Gerber

LENORE BLANK KELNER is a dramatist who works with children of all ages. One day she arrived at an early childhood classroom and was surprised to see the room decorated. Something special was happening. When the children gathered, their teacher said, "Today we are celebrating 100 days of being a school family."

The children looked at various groupings of 100 objects, and then Lenore led them in drama activities. Later, she had a chance to talk with the teacher.

"I can't tell the kids that their families are bad," the teacher said, "although most of them come from difficult backgrounds, filled with hurt and neglect."

The teacher paused. "I can't change the way these kids see life. But I can offer them a second choice. Life doesn't have to be the way they've known it up 'til now, and they have to feel that in their bones.'

There are many ways to build kindness, but the first is the most important, the easiest to understand, and the hardest to change. It's role modeling. If you want to encourage kindness, you have to act kindly. It's pretty hard to encourage kindness if you're not living that way. You don't have to be perfect, but the more kindly you act, the more the children around you will also be kind.

We learn by copying. Whether it's a skill, a process, or an emotional pattern, what children experience from the adults around them is the primary way they learn. When kids come from families that treat each other well, they receive good role modeling. But every class has several—and sometimes a majority—of kids who weren't raised in a peaceful environment.

One original meaning of the Middle English root word "gecynde" has to do with property acquired at or derived from birth. A person's quality comes from the influence of family. It's difficult, but not impossible, to be kind when you're raised in the midst of unkindness.

Our modeling of kindness won't in itself be enough to teach children, but it is an essential ingredient.

In addition, as Alfie Kohn has written, it may be that our job is not only to internalize good values in a community, but also to internalize the value of community itself. Generosity, helpfulness, listening, compassion, and gratitude don't exist alone; they require connection to a community. When we value community itself, our actions flow from a deep-seated set of feelings that are larger than any one person. When adults model participation in a community, they pass these values along to children.

As Gandhi said, "You must be the change you want to see in the world."

PROFESSIONALISM

Children have never been very good at
listening to their elders, but they have
never failed to imitate them.

James Baldwin

GOALS FOR THIS CHAPTER

✳ Consider how professionalism in early childhood impacts kindness.

✳ Recognize that an organization plays a role in promoting kindness.

✳ Consider the role of classroom environments in supporting positive social interactions.

WHEN MY WIFE Heather took a job as director of a childcare center, she learned new lessons about the importance of professionalism. She came from a background in public elementary schools, but now she supervised teachers who had little training and often little commitment to the work. Building a sense of professionalism was one of the tasks she focused on. Many people who worked for her, and who work in the field, do not think of themselves as professionals.

Professionalism implies an ongoing commitment to a career or vocation. Professionals want to improve, learn, and meet high standards in their work. While the expectations of professionals are high, so is the respect they are accorded.

It's common knowledge that the field of early childhood education has its own unique pressures. Workers are typically underpaid, a workday is filled with active children—each demanding or needing individual attention—and often parents bring their own issues during drop-off or pick-up. Childcare is a difficult job, and the lack of appreciation for it is completely at odds with its importance. We should be devoting the best of our resources and respect to the early years.

These realities can strain relationships among co-workers, between supervisors and employees, and with parents. Kindness matters in how we work with one another.

Kindness isn't just about the way we treat children, or the way they treat each other. It's also about the way we as adults treat each other. Children pay careful attention to how we interact with co-workers or parents.

Appreciation

During her long educational career, my wife Heather has held positions as a teacher, a principal, and a university professor. One of the many lessons I drew from her work at a childcare center was about appreciation. Heather made time for noticing, complimenting, and thanking the teachers on a regular basis. She sent notes and emails and said things in the halls to draw attention to good things that teachers did.

Hers was a combination of genuine caring and deliberate ongoing intention and routine. When she talked with staff at other centers, she was always surprised at how little appreciation they received. Heather felt the rise in morale in her center as tangibly as holding an apple in her hand. The atmosphere improved, and turnover, that dreaded scourge of the profession, declined.

Notes, positive comments, and emotional affect are all ways to show that you notice the good work others are doing around you. Don't be afraid of being obvious or explicit; just say something when you see it.

KINDNESS & SCIENCE

A research study measuring job satisfaction demonstrated the powerful effects of appreciation in the workplace. Being appreciated and receiving regular positive feedback had a greater impact than salary. While that may not be too surprising, one unexpected finding showed that job satisfaction was lower when workers received no feedback than when they received regular negative comments. Being noticed was better than being invisible, even if the noticing wasn't pleasant.

When co-workers recognize each other's contributions, work morale improves, partially compensating for poor pay and lack of recognition from the outside world. I believe that people in the early childhood field should be much better compensated than they are. But I also believe that they should be appreciated more, and one place to start is by appreciating one another.

Teachers can demonstrate appreciation to parents for their children, as well. Denise Lew, a teacher in Switzerland, sends 'Glad Notes' to parents to let them know of positive things their child has done. She also uses these opportunities to thank the parents for their support in their child's learning, helping to build bridges with parent partners whenever possible.

Daily Interactions

The way that teachers interact with each other says a lot more than all the lectures, stories, and feel-good posters on the wall.

In addition, the way that teachers and parents interact also paints an evocative picture for children who witness these conversations. Mutual respect and kindness are essential. I've heard many stories about parents who don't respect their children's caregivers and teachers, and vice versa.

Examine your own attitudes and actions with others in your work. Complaining, judging, and insulting are never useful behaviors, and they can poison the well of shared relationships.

Classroom Environment

Teachers can make decisions about classroom environments to promote healthy social interaction. The emotional environment should be safe, with opportunities to share feelings and resolve conflict. Routines like morning meeting and creating classroom agreements about behavior allow everyone to have a chance to be heard.

A classroom's physical structure also affects how children interact and show kindness. Some considerations include:

1. Separating noisy and quiet centers so that children aren't stressed or distracted by interactions around them.

2. Having enough toys and manipulatives that children aren't frustrated by waiting a long time to play with an item.

3. Making sure there's enough space for a variety of activities.

4. Displaying posters or other images that show children sharing and getting along.

5. Providing access to sunlight and the out-of-doors, thereby allowing children connection with the natural world.

6. Strict limiting of technology, television, and screens of any kind.

In *Yes!* Magazine writer Lennon Flower examined three successful approaches to social-emotional learning for young children. She concluded by writing that the approaches, "Have less to do with what students are taught than with the relationships between children and adults, teacher professional development, school-wide disciplinary practices, and the underlying culture of a school."

Mission and Advocacy

Teachers can share their focus on teaching kindness with parents to encourage connections with the classroom and perhaps influence what occurs at home. Many parents are longing to know more about what happens during the day with their children, and they are also often looking to improve their own skills and understanding.

Administrators can work to incorporate kindness into the larger perspective. They can include references to caring in a mission statement, stated goals and objectives, and evaluations of children's progress. They can offer trainings and opportunities for staff to explore and share ways to build kindness, and they can communicate with parents on a regular basis about the center's or school's emphasis on kindness as a core value.

Another way that teachers can impact kindness in the classroom is by standing up for children. At times teachers may take out their frustration, impatience, or exhaustion on children. While this may not constitute abuse or a reportable incident, it's unacceptable. Teachers may need to talk to coworkers, advocating for and insisting that children are treated with kindness. They may also need to advocate for children in response to parent behavior.

We should not tolerate unkindness toward children. Children may need firm limits and clear feedback, and may even need to be physically removed or restrained in extreme cases, but those are not excuses for unkindness.

Our job is to be there for children first. That's the mark of an early childhood professional.

CHAPTER SUMMARY

1. Teachers who work with young children need to consider themselves as professionals.

2. The environment and interactions between teachers, administrators, and parents affect perceptions and attitudes of children.

3. While kindness is important for children and classrooms, it can also be embedded in educational philosophies, policies, and standards.

4. Adults may need to stand up on behalf of children who are treated badly.

BEAUTY AND WONDERMENT

Let the beauty we love be what we do.
There are hundreds of ways to kneel
and kiss the ground.

Rumi

GOALS FOR THIS CHAPTER

✳ Consider the role of beauty in fostering kindness.

✳ Recognize that the definition of beauty is expansive.

✳ Learn ways to help children appreciate beauty, alone
and with others.

NOTICING BEAUTY IS a way of slowing down, and anything that helps us slow down and live more in the present is a good thing. Kindness is not nurtured by speed.

Children are often more observant than adults. Kafka acknowledged this when he wrote, "Anyone who keeps the ability to see beauty never grows old." We can encourage children's capacity to notice and take joy in simple moments of beauty.

Noticing beauty with others is a connector. When someone draws your attention to something beautiful, not only do you stop, but you also sense an affiliation with that person. You share a moment.

In particular, every face has its own beauty. The stories that lie below the surface of the skin shape that beauty, and when we notice it in others, we can connect with them and build a sense of empathy.

We also have an opportunity to confront and explore cultural notions of beauty—for instance, the message young girls receive about body size and shape, as well as makeup and dress styles. We should be vigilant in facing these issues with children.

Childcare expert Deb Schein wrote an eye-opening doctoral dissertation. She conducted a grounded quantitative research study on teachers who worked with kids. She ran a data search to find patterns in how her teachers described the experience. She found that the key to developing kindness in children was developing the spiritual side of each child.

The moment I heard that I got nervous. Using the word "spiritual" is a lightning rod in our country because of political and religious divisions, so we have to consider carefully what she means by the term.

Her understanding is drawn from Maria Montessori, who lived when microscopes were just becoming available. For the first time, an average person could peer into the tiny world only strong lenses could reveal. Examining a seed, Maria perceived how the embryo or germ grew into a plant and remarked on the similarity to people. Babies are like embryos in seeds, with a certain genetic predisposition. A corn kernel will grow into a plant and become a certain kind of corn; its genes determine that it will probably be tall, or have three ears. Wind and rain will affect it, too, but it will never become a rice plant or an apple tree.

She believed that children are born with certain innate predispositions shaped by genetics and time in the womb, and that the job of a teacher consisted of encouraging the discovery, affirmation, and nurture of those predispositions in healthy directions. She referred to these predispositions as "spirits."

If adults foster these spirits, children can move from being only inner-directed (or ego-centric) to also being outer-directed. The ability to be outer-directed makes kindness possible. Once children feel their basic spirits affirmed, more complex dispositions, including empathy, can blossom.

In other words, when your own needs are met, it's easier to meet the needs of others. In this case, the need isn't for food or shelter but for being essentially recognized and encouraged. Maslow's hierarchy of needs isn't just about shelter and food.

In her research, Deb found that in situations where teachers reported that this "spiritual" recognition occurred, classrooms exhibited more kindness, as shown by behavior and incidents of sharing. The heart of her dissertation proposes that, **"Anything that brings a sense of wonderment and awe creates an environment that facilitates kindness."**

Childcare expert Ruth Wilson echoed Deb's work when she wrote, "Soul-making experiences leave little room for the growth and festering of a constant state of anger and frustration experienced by many children in today's society who do not have frequent positive interactions with the natural world."

We can recognize spirits in a child through moments of beauty. Teachers can regularly give children the chance to stop and notice beauty and experience what Deb calls "wonderment."

 # Rocks

Gather some rocks, palm-sized or smaller. Make it clear that the rocks are for observing but not throwing.

Choose a rock and pass it around a circle of children. Let each child take time to examine it. You may need to pass several rocks at once, so that children don't have to wait too long. Children can share their observations and wonder.

Music

After an active time, have children sit on a rug or even lie down. Gather their ideas about what makes a beautiful piece of music. Their answers will vary. Choose four different pieces from a variety of styles, and have the kids reflect on what they hear. The purpose is to get children to listen more deeply and carefully and to slow down.

Visual Art

Show children a few paintings in an art book, on a computer, or projected on a screen. Just as in the music activity, focus on what they observe rather than on evaluating the work. Encourage them to notice color, texture, and shape. Let them look closely at a work of art, allowing its particular beauty to seep in.

Outdoors

Find beauty in an outdoor setting. Look at something as simple as the inside of a tulip or a variegated leaf changing colors in the fall. Find a grandiose view from a hill overlooking a lake or a tree growing on a city street. Have children stop to notice and appreciate what they see. Urban scenes offer their own variety of beauty.

Pairs

Once you've introduced them to this way of looking and listening, try any of these activities in pairs. Let children look or listen together to a piece of art and share with each other what they hear or see. Appreciating and exploring beauty can strengthen relationships between people.

Who You Are

Have children discuss, draw, or otherwise explore how their reactions, likes, dislikes, or interests in response to any of the above activities reveal something about who they are and how their reactions are both unique and similar to others.

REFLECTIONS·REFLECTIONS·REFLECTIONS·REFLECTIONS

Reflections for Children

1. What happens when you stop and look at something for a long time?

2. What's one thing you noticed today that's new?

3. What's the difference between being inside and outdoors?

Reflections for Adults

1. What do you find beautiful?

2. What do you notice about children as they deeply consider an object or scene and focus on its beauty?

3. How can you encourage and allow time for wonder and awe during the day?

CHAPTER SUMMARY

1. Taking time to focus on beauty creates an atmosphere conducive to kindness.

2. Our definition of beauty can grow beyond what seems obvious or culturally learned.

3. We can encourage children's natural sense of wonder and expect that greater kindness is the likely result.

4. Beauty and wonder are all around us.

POSITIVITY

You've got to accentuate the positive
eliminate the negative
Latch on to the affirmative
But don't mess with Mister In-Between.

Johnny Mercer and Harold Arlen

GOALS FOR THIS CHAPTER

✳ Consider the importance of attitude.

✳ Learn ways to focus on being positive.

✳ Learn strategies to change negative feelings.

EVERY MORNING IN an early childhood classroom in Arizona all the students gather in a circle and hold hands. One by one they take turns naming a goal for the day. Their intentions range from making a tall structure from blocks to playing in the grocery store center with a friend. The teacher gently directs them to think about their goals for working together, for getting along, and for being kind to each other, while also recognizing the importance of giving each child ownership and choice in the process. The responses turn deeper and more serious, highlighting ongoing issues and friendship struggles.

The next routines of the day begin with a whirlwind of motion, including large group activities, free play, exploration areas, snack, and rest time.

At the end of the day the children gather again, holding hands and looking around the circle at one another. One by one each child remembers what their goal was for the day and then says how they did on it. Most of the children find some success in their efforts, and for those who don't, there's always tomorrow.

Positive feelings and emotions foster kindness. Happy classrooms are kinder. An attitude of warmth and ability leads to confidence and smooth interactions. Focusing on what kids can do—rather than what they can't or shouldn't do—creates a healthy emotional environment. We don't want children to "live down" to our expectations.

Teachers set the tone of the classroom. They can direct it in a positive way through activities, expressions, and attitude. They also bear the responsibility for quickly changing the tone when it turns sour.

In addition, teachers set the tone for relationships with each child.

Often teachers undergo training about child development, nutrition, behavior management, literacy foundations, and more. But there's rarely training in the power of joyfulness, and there's no substitute for it. Crabbiness might seem like a successful trait for club bouncers or CEOs, but it is definitely not good for teachers.

Or, as Martin Charnin wrote in Annie, "You're never fully dressed without a smile."

We're wired to pay more attention to unkindness than kindness, so we need to overcompensate. Our natural inclination is to notice threat and conflict more than safety or comfort. We can deliberately cultivate kindness by looking for and focusing on positive aspects and actions.

Encouraging play also makes for a positive classroom. Fun should be fundamental in every young child's life. Over the last few years there has been a concerted push in the field of early childhood to encourage and allow free play for kids, a trend I strongly support. We can expect that imaginative play will increase the incidence of kindness in classrooms.

And then there's laughter, the fuel for joy. Not laughter at someone else's expense but laughter about silliness, play, and delight. Kids love to laugh. **Laugh often, be silly, appreciate their silliness, and let the little things be funny.** Like touch and stories, laughter binds people together, creating trust, warmth, and enough positive feeling to lift the room right off the ground.

K I N D N E S S & S C I E N C E

Science has acknowledged the power of laughter. One study found, "Laughter has shown physiological, psychological, social, spiritual, and quality-of-life benefits. Adverse effects are very limited, and laughter is practically lacking in contraindications. Therapeutic efficacy of laughter is mainly derived from spontaneous laughter (triggered by external stimuli or positive emotions) and self-induced laughter (triggered by oneself at will), both occurring with or without humor. The brain is not able to distinguish between these types; therefore, it is assumed that similar benefits may be achieved with one or the other...this review concludes that there exists sufficient evidence to suggest that laughter has positive, quantifiable effects on aspects of health."

In my years of working with children, their laughter has fed my spirits many times. Laughing together builds connection, trust, and an atmosphere where kindness is welcome.

The Power of Laughter

There are laughing clubs all over the world. People gather in a park, church, or neighborhood center and laugh. They start out by faking it, making themselves laugh, but the group energy soon transforms forced laughter to real laughter.

Try this with kids. Get them started with deliberate laughs, and soon genuine laughter will break out. You have to model this well and give yourself to the laughter completely.

What's interesting about the above study is that self-induced laughter shows the same benefits as spontaneous laughter. When laughter clubs put this idea into practice, there's a scientific basis for its effectiveness.

Songs

Learn or play the song "I Can Do It, Yes I Can." Have kids contribute ideas about what they can do and incorporate actions to illustrate their ideas.

Practice Reset

When the feeling in the room becomes tense or filled with conflict, stop action, have everyone take three breaths, or close their eyes, or sit down. This isn't a punishment or class timeout; it's a pause to change the energy. Some classes have a reset chime or soft whistle.

Teach children the word "reset," although many of them may already know it from technology. It's a technique for a classroom, but also for a child, and it isn't about punishment or consequence. "Reset" gives everyone the opportunity to take responsibility for changing his or her inner orientation.

Affirmations

The power of affirmation plays a role in the success of many sports champions, business executives, and other high achievers. Focusing on repeating simple phrases about desired personal qualities or specific goals can help to rewire the brain.

Interrupting

Many of us have patterns of negativity—for instance, the chronic complainer, the constant victim, or the tattletale. Teachers can discuss the idea of interrupting a negative and useless thought pattern. When negativity manifests, children will have some preparation and understanding of why they are being redirected when they appear to be stuck.

Redirection can involve simply changing the subject, declaring a topic off limits for a short time, or pointing out a negative pattern and asking a child how they are going to change it. Advance discussions help with this approach.

Reflections for Children

1. What does it feel like inside after you've finished laughing?

2. When you are feeling crabby, how do you change?

3. Who is the happiest person you know?

4. How does it feel to be around someone who is often crabby and negative? (Don't let this devolve into blaming someone in the group.)

Reflections for Adults

1. Children can be a delight. They can also be, uh, challenging. What do you do to maintain or create a positive attitude?

2. Who is the most positive person you know? Why? How does it feel to be around that person?

3. How do you help others maintain a positive outlook?

4. What are effective strategies to interrupt repetitive negative thinking?

CHAPTER SUMMARY

✳ **Kindness is nurtured in positive environments and with positive outlooks.**

✳ **Awareness of the importance of attitude should impact behavior.**

✳ **Laughing together is good for everyone.**

✳ **Sometimes people need help to recognize or get unstuck from negative thinking.**

LANGUAGE

Kindness in words creates confidence.
Kindness in thinking creates profoundness.
Kindness in giving creates love.

Lao Tzu

GOALS FOR THIS CHAPTER

✳ Explore how language shapes our understanding of kindness.

✳ Learn how language can help or hinder kindness.

✳ Reflect on how we use language with children.

IF YOU'VE EVER eavesdropped on a two-year old playing alone, you know how young children talk to themselves or hold conversations with people who are not actually in the room. They're thinking out loud. Gradually that process becomes internal as language develops into a vehicle for thought. How we use language is critical for all learning, and in particular, there's a powerful connection to kindness.

Lev Vygotsky was an influential Russian thinker, writer, and psychologist in the early 1900s. He helped shape our modern understanding of how children learn, paying particular attention to language development. He said that language in children begins as an external process that gradually becomes internal by the time a child goes to school.

Our job is to give children the ability to name and notice their feelings so that language can become a way for them to process, accept, and change the inner emotional life that impacts how they respond to and treat others. Noticing verbal, facial, and postural cues leads to naming related feelings so that change can occur.

The words we use make a difference.

Talk about the action or behavior, not the person. Don't say, "You're a hard worker" or "You're a bad kid." Instead, say, "I see you working hard on that sand castle" or "It was very hurtful when you kicked Andy." Drawing the distinction between behavior and personal characteristic is essential. Behavior can change. It's much harder to change who you are.

Move beyond the words "nice" and "mean." Nice seems namby-pamby and vague, while kind holds a certain active power. Mean implies character more than action, and rude is more about behavior. Someone is more likely to act rude, but be perceived as being mean.

Author Carol McCloud has promoted empowering language around kindness. Schools, classrooms, and teachers around the world have adopted the idea of "Bucket Filling." In essence, our positive sense of self is seen as something that can be filled or emptied by our own and others' actions. When we do something kind or helpful, we fill another's bucket. Children respond to and incorporate this idea in their own conceptions of kindness and in their conversations, and teachers can utilize this vocabulary to help children reflect on their actions and interactions.

Leslie Leline, a childcare teacher in Door County, Wisconsin, makes the case for verbalizing the rationale and thinking behind what we see and do, so that children can acquire the words to help them conceptualize what they are feeling and seeing. For example, upon seeing someone share his or her time in the kitchen area, Leslie might say, "When I saw you invite Kayla to play, that seemed like a very kind thing to do, and I saw Kayla looking really happy to be included." In this way, children learn to put words to actions and situations.

Leslie also believes that children can handle sophisticated concepts and vocabulary. Identifying emotions is one area where children may even outpace their adult companions. Her preschoolers learn that it is perfectly normal human behavior to sometimes feel angry, frustrated, crabby, or annoyed, but that it is important to know what to do in those situations. The mother of a three-year old called Leslie and asked incredulously (and happily), "I just heard my daughter say, 'I'm feeling really frustrated right now and I need to go to my room until I'm not feeling so crabby.' What are you teaching these kids?"

The words we use help children figure out who they are. Childcare teachers and providers can change the vocabulary that children have in their heads, which is often negatively charged. Children can carry this form of vocabulary replacement with them for the rest of their lives. In order for this strategy to work, teachers must learn to identify and manage their own emotions first, if they expect children to be able to do so as well.

Praise is a touchy subject. While it's important to maintain a positive view, the ultimate goal is for children to internalize their motivation and understanding, not to please the adults around them. Children naturally want to please, and that's a powerful motivation for them to act kindly. But as they grow, kindness needs to come from someplace deeper, more internal, and more connected to who they are.

One solution is to thank children for behavior rather than praising. "Thank you for helping Maia to pick up the sand toys. That was helpful for her and for me." It's subtly different from saying, "I liked how you helped" or, "You are such a good girl for helping."

Another approach is to notice and connect to the child's inner sense of self. "You must have felt good when you helped..." In that case you are providing the words to help them understand themselves and directing attention toward kindness.

We can notice kindness in others and in ourselves, using language to process and change our understanding.

 # Noticing and Responding

Children can identify when they feel frustrated or angry. That's when rudeness is more likely to occur. They may benefit from learning a process.

1. Notice when you are feeling frustrated or angry.

2. Put your hand over your mouth.

3. Take deep breaths and walk away.

4. Come back when you are feeling better.

It's helpful to practice this strategy in a time of neutral emotion. Children need ways to regulate their own emotions. The time an emotion lingers by itself in our brains is very short, but when we hold on to it or can't let go, the consequences can last a lifetime.

It's also good to help children identify physical responses associated with emotions: tight stomach, clenched jaw, or avoiding eye contact.

 # Listing Behavior

Make a list of ten kind and unkind behaviors. Don't focus on any child or any recent or ongoing interaction. This is not a chance to process problems but to think on a larger scale. This activity allows children to build vocabulary to address and assess situations later.

 # Listing Feeling Words

Make a list of words that describe how someone feels when they've acted kindly, and how they feel when they have been recipients of a kind action. Make a second list of feeling words that relate to how it feels to be treated unkindly. Again, don't let the list get personal or specific to anyone.

Turtle

Have every child sit on the carpet. Ask them to curl themselves into the shape of a turtle, with their head tucked in. Have them sit up again. Explain that when they are feeling crabby they can become like a turtle, going inside their shell and taking deep breaths until they are ready to speak positively again. They don't need to actually assume the form of a turtle when they are crabby. They can merely withdraw until their attitude has changed.

REFLECTIONS•REFLECTIONS•REFLECTIONS•REFLECTIONS

Reflections for Children

1. What are some words for emotions you might feel?

2. What words do we use when someone is being unkind?

3. What do you notice in your body when you are feeling frustrated or angry?

Reflections for Adults

1. How were feelings handled or discussed in your family of origin?

2. Are you able to identify your feelings when you are working with children?

3. What kinds of physical clues do you notice in children that show you how they are feeling?

CHAPTER SUMMARY

✳ **How we use language shapes how children understand kindness.**

✳ **We can encourage children to notice their feelings rather than simply reacting.**

✳ **Often children may notice what's happening in their bodies before they can name their emotions.**

LISTENING

Our listening creates a sanctuary for the
homeless parts within another person.

Rachel Naomi Remen

GOALS FOR THIS CHAPTER

✱ Children will improve their ability to listen and pay attention to others.

✱ Children will listen for comprehension and meaning.

✱ Children will experience positive feelings from listening and from being listened to.

EBBY MELAHN, a teacher in Saudi Arabia, had a preschool child come up to her one morning and tell her that he had done something nice. When she inquired, he said that he had asked someone how she was feeling. Ebby replied that that was something nice that many adults often do, too.

"Yes," he said, "but I really listened when she told me."

Listening is an essential life skill that improves with practice. It's also essential for kindness. On the wall in an early childhood center I read, "Sometimes the experience of being listened to is indistinguishable from the experience of being loved." Merely listening to someone may be a huge act of kindness in itself.

How we model listening is critical, but listening also has lasting relationship implications for children. Writer and teacher Catherine Wallace advises parents, "Listen earnestly to anything your children want to tell you, no matter what. If you don't listen eagerly to the little stuff when they are little, they won't tell you the big stuff when they are big, because to them, all of it has always been big."

We teach listening so that children can learn the norms and expectations of conversation and the give and take of attention. We also teach it so that children can understand and feel understood by others.

Listening often seems to be in short supply. The writer Ernest Hemingway said, "I like to listen. I have learned a great deal from listening carefully. Most people never listen."

Listening is a fundamental way to learn, but we rarely teach the skill explicitly. Technology has also degraded our ability to listen to each other. We often trade the messy intimacy of conversation for updates, posts, and tweets. Listening takes patience. It means putting aside to-do lists, phones, and the multiple demands on our attention in our modern lives and simply focusing on the person, child, or adult, who is talking with us.

Some important considerations:

1. Get down at a child's physical level. Listening occurs between equals.
2. Ask a child to repeat back what you have said in their own words to show that they have understood.

3. Work on listening in small amounts of time.

4. Make the content interesting and relevant. We don't need to teach them to listen to something that's inherently boring. They'll get plenty of that later in high school.

KINDNESS & SCIENCE

Brown University neuroscientist Seth Horowitz says, "While it might take you a full second to notice something out of the corner of your eye, turn your head toward it, recognize it, and respond to it, the same reaction to a new or sudden sound happens at least 10 times as fast." Horowitz says hearing has evolved as a more essential tool for survival than sight.

Room sounds

Sit in a circle and ask for absolute quiet. Have children notice what sounds they hear in the natural background of the room: clock ticking, cars outside, or voices in the hall. Listen for thirty seconds and have children list what they heard. Be prepared for an outbreak of giggles. We're not used to being silent, and the resulting sense of discomfort may provoke laughter.

Taking turns

In pairs, have one child talk for fifteen seconds, while the second child does nothing but listen. Switch roles. Switch partners. Reflect with children about their experience.

Story

Tell them a story, but insert things that don't fit or couldn't be true. "I was walking down the street and a cow flew by." Have children raise their hands when they hear something that doesn't fit.

Simon Says

Simon Says is a time-tested game to improve kids' listening. Give them actions to do, but instruct them to only do them if preceded by the words, "Simon says." You will find that their focus and listening increases as you play.

Talking Stick

There are cultures in the world that use some form of the "talking stick" in meetings or conversations. An object, which doesn't have to be a stick, is placed in the center of the circle or at the front of the room. The person who has the object is the only one allowed to talk. Everyone else has the responsibility of listening. Teachers may need to ensure that children share the stick and that everyone has equal access to it.

The talking stick helps children monitor their own participation, and it teaches listening.

Talking Chits

In any group discussion, it's important that a few children don't dominate the conversation and that everyone has an equal chance to share.

Create talking chits. Use playing cards, index cards, or Popsicle sticks. Distribute an equal number to each child, perhaps 3-5. Each time someone shares, they put one of their chits into the center, perhaps into a pot or box. When a child runs out of chits, they can't speak again until more chits are distributed.

This activity helps children to monitor their own and others' participation in discussion.

Mouth and Ears

Have children work in pairs to tell a story from a picture book or from their own lives. Each pair has two cards or papers. One card has the picture of a mouth, and the other has a picture of an ear.

Explain that ears don't talk, they only listen.

Have the child who holds the image of the mouth begin telling their story to their partner. After a designated time, say "Switch" and have the children exchange cards, giving the other partner the opportunity to talk and the first child the expectation of listening. The first rule is that only the person with the "mouth" card can talk. The second rule is that the person with the "ear" card is expected to listen carefully.

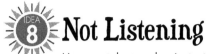

Not Listening

Have a volunteer begin to tell you about something they know well, e.g., describing their bedroom. Do everything you can to be a poor listener: look the other way, pretend to look on a smartphone, look at your shoe, look out the window, etc. Have children identify these behaviors. Then repeat with a different volunteer, but this time with positive, active listening behaviors.

REFLECTIONS•REFLECTIONS•REFLECTIONS•REFLECTIONS

Reflections for Children

1. What did you hear when you sat quietly in the room? Was it hard to sit and just listen?

2. When someone else is talking, are you listening to what they are saying or thinking about what you want to say back?

3. What do you have to do to play *Simon Says* successfully?

Reflections for Adults

1. What did you notice about children as they engaged in the activities?

2. How else have you taught listening skills to students in the past?

3. Who listens well to you?

4. Who do you enjoy listening to?

CHAPTER SUMMARY

✳ Listening is an essential skill for success, and even for survival.

✳ Children can learn to listen more effectively and learn from others by doing so.

✳ Listening provides a way to understand and to be understood.

EMPATHY AND COMPASSION

Compassion is not weakness, and concern
for the unfortunate is not socialism.

Hubert H. Humphrey

GOALS FOR THIS CHAPTER

✳ Learn the difference between empathy and compassion
and how they are related.

✳ Discover activities to build empathetic awareness.

✳ Appreciate ways to encourage compassionate
responses.

IN A CLASSROOM in North Carolina, a teacher named Maria watched as Devonne sat by himself, surrounded by pillows, his knees pulled up to his chest. It was his second week in the four-year old room, and things had not been going well.

Maria saw Bianca, another four-year old, approach Devonne cautiously. He looked up at her, and she handed him a plastic flower from the kitchen play area.

"I hope you feel better," she said.

He took the flower and smiled for the first time that day.

Empathy is the ability to put oneself in another's shoes, to understand how someone else is feeling. For example, when a child is mistreated, we might feel some moral outrage, but we can also imagine how the child feels, based on our own experience. In the same way, when someone wins a game, we can experience joy and triumph in part because we can recall or sense how we would feel in that situation.

Empathy is a key ability for deep kindness, because we are moved not by duty or habit, but by connection and emotion. We can't maintain distance and remain unaffected when we feel someone else's pain.

Compassion takes empathy a step further, adding the desire to help or relieve suffering. One dictionary defines compassion as, "Deep awareness of the suffering of another coupled with the wish to relieve it." Compassion is an active response to hurt.

In a sense, empathy is an emotional intelligence, and compassion is the impulse to connect and help once you feel someone else's pain.

Compassion and empathy are different from pity. Pity implies a sense of looking down on someone's suffering or seeing it as separate from what you know.

With compassion we reach out from an empathetic experience. We recognize that life is hard for others. Plato said, "Be kind, for everyone you meet is fighting a harder battle." Compassion means reaching beyond our own suffering to encounter another's with gentleness and care.

Start with children learning to name and process their own feelings. The ability to simply notice and name any given feeling is a foundation for empathy. Once children have accessed their own emotional vocabulary it will be easier for them to empathize and recognize others' emotions. Use kinesthetic and facial expressions as well as words to access emotions.

KINDNESS & SCIENCE

"While there are some indications that infants sense when others are stressed and react to the situation with concern, the ability to actually understand the feelings and emotions of others is acquired at a later stage in a child's development (Roffey, 2006)."

We can build empathy through stories. Children can relate to how a character might feel and can express that feeling in their own bodies. In successful fiction and film, a key question is whether an audience identifies with the characters and feels empathy for their situations and conflicts.

When children empathize, they can look beyond themselves. They begin to realize that they are not the center of the universe. They are ready to experience compassion.

Face

Facial expression is one of storytelling's key elements. It's also a way to help children get in touch with emotion.

1. **Mirror circle.** Have children sit in front of you in a circle or a U, so that they can all easily see your face. Make a dramatic face of any kind (silly, scared, angry, excited) and ask them to mirror the face back to you, freezing their faces until you tell them to let go or relax. Look at children's faces to assess how well they mirrored and to appreciate them all for trying. Once they have relaxed, ask them what kind of feelings the face expresses. Have them make the face again after having identified the emotion.

2. **Tell or read a story.** At different points during the story, have students show you with their faces what they think a character is feeling. Then add words to identify the feeling.

3. **Eye Contact.** In this activity children experience how it feels to talk and listen both with and without eye contact. Begin by modeling. Work with one volunteer. Instruct that child to look at you while you talk. Talk about any appropriate subject for 15 seconds, but do not look at the child. When you stop, ask the child and the rest of the group what they perceived and how they imagine it would have felt to listen to someone who was not looking at you.

4. Repeat the process, but this time look at the child while you are talking. Reflect with the group on the effect of conversing with eye contact.

5. **Have children work in pairs.** Provide an easy way to divide them up: A and B, X and Y, Red and Green, etc. Let them try the activity, with each child taking turns talking and listening. Time the conversations to last no more than 15 seconds. Reflect with them again on their feelings during the different stages of the activity.

6. Provide a scenario for the talker such as falling down on the playground, getting hit by another child, missing their mother, wanting to keep playing when playtime is over. Have the talker tell what has happened and lead the listener through the story.

7. Reverse roles, and then change partners with a different scenario.

Voice and Face

Say a feeling with an opposite face, for example, "I'm so happy" while making an angry face. Other possibilities include: happy/sad, tired/excited, scared/happy, mad/sad, surprised/bored. Have children do the same with a partner.

Stop, Breathe, Listen, Respond

This activity comes from Girls on the Run in North Carolina, an organization that works to empower girls' life skills and physical activity.

Introduce the situation of a friend coming to talk with you about something that has upset them. Role-play the following steps.

1. Stop and focus on the friend.

2. Take a breath to calm yourself.

3. Listen without interrupting.

4. Ask the friend how they are feeling and ask what you can do to help.

5. Have children work in pairs. Identify one as the listener and the other as the talker.

In Your Shoes

Get four shoeboxes and put very different shoes in them: business shoes, tennis shoes, baby shoes, ballet slippers, etc. You can find used shoes at a resale shop for this purpose. (Sanitizing shoes may be important, depending on where you get them. You can also show images of shoes instead of using the real items.)

Explain that empathy is about feeling what someone else is feeling, i.e., "walking in someone else's shoes."

Have one child come forward and choose a box. Open the box and reveal the shoes inside. Have that child put on the shoes. Each shoebox contains a written scenario that tells something about a character and a story. For example, ballet slippers might include a story about someone being too sick to be in the ballet performance. Tennis shoes might be about someone who goes to play ball but doesn't get picked for the team.

Once you've read the scenario, ask the child in the shoes how they would feel if it were their story. Other children may also contribute ideas about feelings.

Reflect on how children imagined themselves in a different situation and connected with the feelings associated with it. This is empathy

Song

Listen to Vitamin L's song "I Want to Walk a Mile In Your Shoes." Learn the chorus and sing along to reinforce the concept of empathy.

REFLECTIONS•REFLECTIONS•REFLECTIONS•REFLECTIONS

Reflections for Children

1. Why is it important to know what others are feeling?

2. How do you feel when someone takes time to care about your feelings? Why?

3. Can we know how someone else feels without using words? How?

Reflections for Adults

1. What is the difference between empathy and compassion?

2. Can you be compassionate without empathy?

3. How did you learn to recognize your own feelings?

4. What's a time someone you know demonstrated empathy and compassion?

CHAPTER SUMMARY

✳ Empathy and compassion are cornerstones of kindness.

✳ Knowing how others feel is important for kindness and also for general social success.

✳ Authentic compassion proceeds from empathy for others.

MANNERS

"Oh Tigger, where are your manners?"
"I don't know, but I bet they're having more fun than I am."

A.A. Milne. Winnie the Pooh

GOALS FOR THIS CHAPTER

* Explore why manners are a foundation of kindness.
* Recognize that manners are not universally consistent—they vary from person to person and culture to culture.
* Learn ways to promote manners among children.

Michelle Watkins is a copywriter and marketing expert. She's also a mother. In her work she often signs her emails with "Thanks" or "Thank you." Most people do that these days, without thinking about it much.

One day she realized she was habitually thanking people in work communications but not so often extending thanks at home. She began to focus on regularly thanking the people in her household.

Over the next few weeks, her children noticed and began being more thankful and polite as well. The feeling in the house as a whole improved.

Manners matter.

Manners and kindness are connected. Kindness is more than manners, but manners are a great place to start. Manners are more than social conventions, as Emily (the Queen of Manners) Post acknowledged when she said, "Manners are a sensitive awareness of the feelings of others. If you have that awareness, you have good manners, no matter which fork you use."

Manners ease social interactions like grease around ball bearings. They round out the edges of everyday exchanges, making shopping, traveling, eating, and entertainment more pleasant.

Manners are like rules, and children need to know the rules. But they also need to understand the reasons behind the rules in order to develop an authentic sense of kindness.

It's our job as adults to teach kids manners. It's one step of initiation on the road to being a competent grown up. We often start by simply having kids insert the right words.

Child reaches across the table: Give me the book.

Adult looks meaningfully from the book to the child, echoing: Give me the book...(Pause)

Child takes the cue: Give me the book, please.

Some form of this dialogue is undoubtedly taking place right now many places on earth. Such an exchange can build a habit of manners. We want kids to reflexively use manners in everyday social interactions. Manners should become instinctive but not lacking in awareness. Kindness and manners go together, but we deepen the experience so that manners provide both social lubricant and emotional significance.

We teach the words, but we can also teach the deeper meaning. We can use drama, role modeling, and role-playing to demonstrate the power of manners, and we can use songs as reminders.

 # Thank you

The word "thank" shares a linguistic origin with the word "think." In this sense, thank means "to have a good thought about." In a small group, identify an act that someone has done for you that you are grateful for. Talk for a short time about why you think well of that person. By turns, have children think about a kind action done for them. Let them talk about their thoughts and feelings about the person who performed the kindness.

 # Role-play

Work with another teacher or a child to role-play situations with and without manners. Focus on the emotional impact of an interaction. Make a request with and without adding "please" at the end. Receive a favor with and without saying "thank you." Have children work in pairs practicing both kinds of interactions.

The caution in this activity is that behaving without manners can seem funny. (And frankly, it is kind of funny when you're pretending.) The challenge is to get children to focus on the deeper emotional response to the lack of and the inclusion of manners.

 # Reasons

Talk with children about any given rule of courtesy, such as saying, "please" or "excuse me." Have them discuss why this rule or habit is a good idea. Extend the discussion to other common courtesies such as raising one's hand or saying "Thank you." Let children grapple with these questions rather than you simply providing answers. Allow a dialogue to occur where questions and answers are considered with openness.

Extending Manners

Ask children if they know other rules or manners they would like to see become part of the classroom environment.

Songs

Songs can reinforce manners. There are many good songs out there. Manners shouldn't feel like drudgery, they should feel like second nature, and singing about them can help build the habit. Links available at **www.StuartStotts.com/kindness-resources.**

Morning Meeting

Responsive Classrooms is an organization that works to promote positive school climate and effective learning. One of their strategies involves holding a daily morning meeting in which students and teachers build relationships with each other. Clarifying expectations for behavior and manners are central to this approach. Being explicit and positive help create a foundation for treating each other kindly and respectfully throughout the day, and beyond.

In a larger sense, Responsive Classrooms has many great ideas that connect to nurturing kindness. Learn more at **www.ResponsiveClassroom.org**.

REFLECTIONS • REFLECTIONS • REFLECTIONS • REFLECTIONS

Reflections for Children

1. Why do manners matter?
2. How does it feel when someone doesn't use manners?
3. Who teaches you manners?

Reflections for Adults

1. Is it enough to teach manners to children?
2. How do you teach manners without lecturing or constantly reminding?
3. Do you notice correlations between children's' manners and those of the grown-ups in their lives?

CHAPTER SUMMARY

✳ Manners matter. They should be instinctive.

✳ Children are more likely to learn manners if they understand reasons for using them.

✳ Manners impact the way we feel.

INCLUSION

I'm gonna sit at the welcome table...

Traditional Spiritual Song

GOALS FOR THIS CHAPTER

✳ Learn ways to help children include each other.

✳ Make connections between exclusive behavior and damaging actions like bullying.

✳ Consider how kindness connects to children with special needs.

MANDY TEACHES AT a preschool in Minnesota. She leans against a tree and observes her class of three and four-year-old kids running wild on the playground. It's a spring day, and wood chips are flying like confetti as kids roll, jump, shout, and laugh.

Four year-old Kendra approaches Mandy, a tear poised on her cheek. She points to a group of children climbing on a plastic structure and whimpers, "They said I can't play." Mandy wipes Kendra's cheek, takes her hand, and walks toward the cluster of kids.

Kindness manifests itself in welcoming and inclusion. Circles, cliques, BFFs, and clubs all become ways to form alliances and exclusive groups. While the consequences for young children are hurtful, these kinds of behaviors can later become a foundation of bullying, when a victim is isolated and targeted. By focusing on inclusion and welcoming, we can begin to address these issues with young children.

Another meaning of inclusion involves how we work with children with special needs. Many teachers have spoken with me about the need for specialized learning for some of the kids in their classes. We know that autism rates are rising and that the labeling of children continues to grow. There are now an ever-increasing variety of categories into which to place challenging children.

Teachers teach kindness to all children. Young children are generally less likely to perceive differences of ability, color, or ethnicity. Educational inclusion offers many opportunities to expand circles of kindness, and kids get to learn about tolerance and compassion.

With learners of any age, teachers have to find the approaches and strategies that work, and we can't make generalizations about teaching to any particular strength or challenge. Whatever the difficulty, kindness practices reach across any spectrum.

Nevertheless, inclusive classrooms may face barriers of space, money, staff time, and prejudice. Children's behaviors may force us to expand our sense of what's acceptable, search deeply for root causes, and recognize that sometimes we can't easily figure out the internal rules a child is living by. Kindness can still remain one of our guiding principles; in fact, it is embedded in the idea of educational inclusion.

Exclusion among young children can create hurt. Children use it to exercise their power, to bond with other children over a common scapegoat, to express preference, and to avoid difficulties with another child. While we might want to honor children's choices, we need to acknowledge that exclusion disturbs an atmosphere of kindness.

KINDNESS & SCIENCE

Neuroscientists in Italy have discovered that "social pain" activates the same brain regions as physical pain. Social pain is caused by events such as exclusion from social connections or activities, rejection, bullying, and the sickness or death of a loved one.

Everyone wants to feel included, and being left out can cause short and long term emotional damage in children throughout school and even into adulthood. The party we are not invited to, the working group we're not in, or even the time we stand at the rope of a dance club, watching others allowed entrance to a fancy event can injure our emotional health.

In Vivien Paley's book *You Can't Say You Can't Play*, she discusses the development and consequences of having a rule that requires inclusion for her kindergarteners. It is as simple in implementation as it sounds. **Children are no longer allowed to tell others that they can't join in play.**

Paley found that once the reasons for the rule had been discussed and children had accepted it, the change was not so difficult, and the resulting emotional atmosphere improved. Before implementing it, she imagined that the rule might require a large transformation, but the actual change was fairly smooth.

Paley writes, "Each time a cause for sadness is removed for even one child, we all rise in stature...When I was in a first-grade classroom 55 years ago, it would have been an enormous relief to me if the fat girl with only one dress had been treated kindly."

In this statement she acknowledges that the pain of exclusion is felt not only by those who are excluded, but also by those who do the excluding. There's an emotional cost paid for being on the inside as well as on the outside.

Young children respond well to the concept of inclusion because the experience of being excluded or included is central to their lives. They recognize the actions and the feelings, and they can make specific changes in response.

You Can't Say. . .

Discuss the "You can't say you can't play" idea with children. Do not allow the conversation to turn into blaming or identifying certain children on either side of the equation. Simply talk about fairness, or the pain and hurt from being excluded, or the conflicts that arise from exclusion. Talk about the idea of shyness as well. Implement the rule, and after a few days, discuss its impact with your class.

In the end, children can learn that despite the short-term gratification that may come from being on the inside, they will feel happier when they are inclusive. As Vivien Grace Paley writes, "Words do make a difference. The children are learning that it is far easier to open the doors than to keep people out."

Books

Read books like *The Mitten* by Jan Brett or *There's Always Room for Just One More* by Sorche Nic Leodhas. Create an enclosed space with string or chairs and act out the stories, making room for everyone by the time the story is done.

Practice

Practice including people. Introduce language to welcome new children into class or activities. Role-play asking someone to take part in a game or group.

Role-play

Role-play situations where one person is excluded. Discuss the feelings that arise as a result. Let children experience the feelings of being left out and have them talk about it. Using facial exercises may help kids explore their feelings more easily.

Photographs

Glue photographs of each child on a small wooden block or cardboard toilet paper roll. Use these objects to create groups, stack structures, or tell stories about relationships and activities and how children can get along.

Walking and Welcoming

Walk with children in the halls of the school and in the streets of the neighborhood with the intention of greeting those you pass with a silent nod, a smile, or a wave, but always including eye contact.

Banner

Children like to contribute to making welcome banners for new students. A large sheet of paper unrolled and filled with drawings, names, and messages of welcome will help any new arrival feel more at home.

Sign Language

Learn sign language for "hello," "come on in," "thank you," "friend," and other words of welcome. Video sign language dictionaries on the Internet demonstrate most common words.

Song

Sing "Come On In" or another welcoming song to begin the day. Insert children's names or details about them to be sure that everyone starts out the day feeling connected to the group.

Reflections for Children

1. Think of a time you've included someone in a group or activity. How did that feel?

2. Did you ever feel excluded? When? What happened?

3. How do you feel when you see someone who wants to be included in a group, but who isn't?

4. What does it take to help someone feel included or welcomed?

Reflections for Adults

1. What are the connections between feeling excluded and bullying behaviors?

2. How much should you intervene to help with inclusion?

3. What are some things you've encountered in working with children with special needs?

CHAPTER SUMMARY

✳ **Feeling welcome is critical to connection, relationship, and community.**

✳ **Children can learn to recognize exclusion, and can learn strategies to help.**

✳ **Everyone benefits from a sense of inclusion.**

FOOD

Be not forgetful to entertain strangers
for thereby some have entertained
angels unawares.

Hebrews 13:2

GOALS FOR THIS CHAPTER

✳ Learn ways to use eating times as opportunities to reinforce kindness.

✳ Discover ways to share food with others.

✳ Teach values of hospitality.

I LOVE TO share a meal in family childcare centers, sitting with eight or ten kids around a common table, passing bowls of food and making conversation. Sometimes it's messy, but I always get the feeling that kids are receiving something profound through the simple act of eating together.

Sharing food with others is one of civilization's oldest acts of kindness. In some cultures, hospitality itself is sacred, and people are enjoined to treat even enemies well when food is involved. Food is central to life everywhere. As master chef and baker James Beard has written, "Food is our common ground, a universal experience."

We know that eating together at home has declined as a family activity. Some families eat out regularly, and others cluster around a television set or eat in shifts to accommodate busy schedules. This makes eating together even more special.

KINDNESS & SCIENCE

A number of studies have found correlations between academic success and family mealtimes. Other studies have found connections to courteous behavior, better diet, and decreased probability of drug or alcohol use.

Kindness and food go together like peanut butter and jelly. Whether we are thinking about eating together, preparing food together, or sharing and offering food to others, the idea of sitting together at a table invokes images of affection and hospitality.

Table Manners

A meal is an excellent time to reinforce and initiate kindness with children. The way we eat together is a crucible of kindness. Manners are essential; passing food, complimenting the cook, holding civil conversations, and using silverware correctly all help to create a pleasant and kind eating experience. Make agreements with children about your shared expectations for manners at meals. Discuss why manners make meals more pleasant, and provide gentle reminders when needed.

Taste

Meals can also be a time to eat mindfully. Help children to savor food and to be aware of where the food comes from and of the people who have played a part in preparing it.

Jon Kabat Zinn is a notable author and teacher of mindfulness. He suggests this raisin meditation as a way to introduce mindfulness, and it might be effective with your children, although if they don't like raisins you should use a different food. Lead children through the following steps.

1. Have children sit comfortably in a chair.
2. Let them take a raisin in hand.
3. Tell them to look carefully at the raisin, as if they'd never seen one before.
4. Have them imagine it growing on the vine. Notice its shape, color, texture, and size.
5. Have them think about where the raisin came from, and the steps it took to get it from the vine to your table. You may need to share some information and pictures about the raisin's journey.
6. Have them smell it.
7. Ask them to notice if they're looking forward to eating the raisin, and if it's hard to not eat it.
8. Have them put the raisin in their mouth, noticing how it feels on their mouth or tongue.
9. Ask them to bite it lightly and then chew three times and stop, noticing what has happened to the raisin.
10. Have them describe how the raisin tastes.
11. Have them chew it slowly and then swallow.
12. Ask them to sit quietly and remember the taste and texture of the raisin.

Care Packages

Create a care package for someone. It might be for a college student, a member of the Armed Services, an older person living nearby, or simply someone you care about.

Have children think about what that person might like and then create the care package based on their ideas. It might include baking something to include or buying a special and rare item.

Care packages bring a personal element to the giving of food.

Food Pantry

In our society, there are always hungry people. Many schools collect food for local food pantries. Have students bring in canned or boxed food, and also other household items like toothpaste or diapers.

Students might benefit from a visit to a food pantry to understand how the process works and put faces on the idea of sharing food this way.

Out to Eat

If you go out to eat in a restaurant, talk with children about being kind to the person waiting on you. Explain that servers deserve to be treated well. Explain the idea of a tip and leave a large one.

Too many people treat food servers poorly. Start kids out right with waiters and waitresses.

The Long Spoons

Every year, care provider Oma Vic McMurray tells the story of "The Long Spoons" to the children in her childcare and follows it with acting out the narrative.

The Long Spoons

A man was given a tour of two places so he could decide where he wanted to live.

In the first room, he saw a lot of people sitting at a long banquet table loaded with delicious food. However, he noticed that all the people seemed unhappy and frustrated. They each had a fork strapped to their left arm and a knife strapped to their right—they had no elbows! Each utensil had a four-foot handle, which made it impossible for them to eat. Even with all kinds of good food in front of them, they couldn't taste any of it.

Next the man was led to a second room. Here the people were also seated at a long banquet table loaded with delicious food. They also had forks and knives with a four-foot handle—and they also had no elbows. However, these people were cheerful and enjoying themselves.

They were busy eating because they were feeding each other. Each person was feeding someone across the table and was being fed in return. The people in the other room were unable to eat because they were trying to feed only themselves.

Where do you think the man chose to live?

After hearing the story, the kids act it out. Oma Vic has some long-handled wooden spoons, and kids sit around the table and feed one another. One of the interesting dynamics occurs when kids of different ages interact—young ones feeding older ones and vice versa.

Oma Vic loves the activity, but she has a few cautions. The first time she tried it, she used long hot-dog forks. Not a great idea to have sharp implements flying around kids' faces. She also makes sure she sets the food up outside, with either easily scooped lunch food or, better yet, ice cream. And of course, good bibs or messy art clothes are best to wear. The kids love feeding each other, and there's lots of laughter, spills, and connection.

Grateful For

At my house, and in many other homes, before eating we go around the table and say at least one thing we are grateful for. The responses might be as simple as the food itself or a good day at school. When my daughter was a teenager and frequently unhappy with her family, she still managed to squeeze out that she was grateful "for her friends."

It's a simple ritual. Some children will copy others' answers. You can vary the order of answering or simply proceed in a circle around the table. Be certain that everyone is listening to each answer as well.

Snack

Many childcare centers and classrooms have snack time. Often children's families may provide snacks as well.

Have the children role-play sharing food so they can identify what feels good in the process as well as what might be hurtful.

Folktales

Many folktales have food as a central theme. From "The Little Red Hen" baking bread to "Cinderella" feeding the birds, how characters deal with food often reveals something essential about the essence of who they are.

The character Nasruddin appears in many Sufi stories from Persia. He plays the role of the wise fool, similar at times to Jack in English or Appalachian stories. Children might enjoy acting a Nasruddin story out, and they can discuss how appearance affects our perception of someone we meet.

Before telling the story you may want to explain to children that Ramadan is a Muslim holiday that lasts for a month. During that holiday, people do not eat while the sun is in the sky; they only eat before the sun rises and after the sun has gone down.

Nasruddin Feeds His Clothes.

Nasruddin had been working in the fields all day. He was tired and sweaty, and his clothes and shoes were covered with mud and stains. Because he had been fasting all day for Ramadan, he was also hungry. As the sun went down, Nasruddin knew that he would soon be able to eat.

The wealthiest man in town had invited everyone to come to his home that evening to break their fasts with a huge feast. Nasruddin knew that he would be late if he went home to change his clothes first. He decided he would rather arrive in dirty clothes than be late. As he walked to the wealthy man's home, Nasruddin imagined the delicious food that he would eat: dates, lentils and chickpeas, olives and bread, hummus, falafel, chicken and beef, and, best of all, the desserts—halvah, date rolls, figs, and baklava.

When Nasruddin arrived, the wealthy man opened the door and looked Nasruddin up and down scornfully, from his worn, ragged hat down to his muddy shoes. Without a word of welcome, he gestured for Nasruddin to enter.

Nasruddin joined the other guests, all dressed in their finest clothing. The tables were filled with the delicious foods he had imagined.

But the seats were all taken and nobody moved to make space for him. No one offered him anything to eat. He had to reach over and around people to get his food. No one even spoke to him. It was as if he wasn't even there.

The other guests ignored him so completely that Nasruddin couldn't enjoy the food on his plate, no matter how tasty it was. In fact, after only a few bites, he felt so uncomfortable that he decided to leave.

He hurried home and changed into his finest clothing, including a beautiful coat.

When he returned back to the feast, the host welcomed him with a huge smile. "Come in, come in." As Nasruddin entered, people waved and called to him from all corners of the room, inviting him to sit near them and offering him food.

Nasruddin sat down quietly. Picking up a plump fig, he carefully placed it into a coat pocket, saying, "Eat, coat, eat." Next he took a handful of nuts and put them into the pocket, saying, "Eat, coat, eat." Then he began to feed his coat in earnest, grabbing all sorts of food.

He fed the coat lentils and chickpeas, olives and bread, hummus, falafel, chicken and beef, and, best of all, the desserts—halvah, date rolls, figs, and baklava.

The guests grew silent as they watched Nasruddin's strange behavior. Soon everyone in the room was staring at him. The host hurried over. "Nasruddin, what are you doing? Why are you feeding your coat?"

"Well," replied Nasruddin, "When I first came to this feast in my old farming clothes, I wasn't welcome. No one would speak with me. But when I changed into this coat, suddenly I was greeted warmly. So I realized it was not I who was welcome at this party, but my clothing. And so I am feeding my coat."

 # Compliments to the Cook

At the end of a meal, take time to deliberately thank the person or people who prepared it. Remark on things you noticed or enjoyed about the food. If the food isn't that good, still recognize the effort people took to make it.

Reflections for Children

1. Why is it important to have good table manners?

2. How does it feel to share food with others?

3. How does it feel when others share food with you?

Reflections for Adults

1. What memories do you have of food and kindness when you were young?

2. How do you observe children relating to food with one another?

3. What do you hope children will learn about food and kindness?

CHAPTER SUMMARY

✳ **Food offers many opportunities to explore kindness.**

✳ **The way we relate to food with others is an indicator of our character.**

KINDNESS AND CULTURE

I think that this whole world
Soon, mama, my whole wide world
Soon gonna be gettin' mixed up.

Pete Seeger

GOALS FOR THIS CHAPTER

✳ Consider the implications of the diverse world we live in.

✳ Recognize that kindness may manifest in different ways in different cultures.

✳ Learn activities to explore language and self-concept as they relate to kindness.

✳ Find activities to explore the gifts of our multi-cultural world.

AN EXTRAORDINARY MIXING of culture, language, and family built the United States, and that process accelerates daily in its speed and variety. This multicultural world is a gift, bringing new learning, food, music, games, and understandings. Sometimes it's a challenge, as well.

We can expect that our classrooms will have children from countries we've barely heard of, speaking languages as varied as flowers in a healthy prairie. Our assumptions and expectations aren't always shared. We can't assume that the traditions and perceptions of kindness will be the same for every culture.

KINDNESS & SCIENCE

Back in 1968 when Crosby, Stills, and Nash sang, "When you smile at me, I will understand, because that is something everybody does in the same language," they were stating a scientific truth. Smiles are recognized everywhere as signs of happiness and welcome, and our brains are hardwired to express and recognize certain feelings through facial expressions.

Because ways of caring and showing connection may vary from place to place, we have to consider what it means to interact in a multicultural classroom. We may have to cope with multiple languages and the emotional challenges of children new to a country and way of life. Children and families navigate their way through different mazes: money, housing, public expectations of behavior, shopping, driving, and more.

Multicultural thinking is not a separate area of its own. It needs to be implicit in every activity. We have to bring an awareness of different needs. The question is always: "Is this student understanding, and if not, what can we do to help?"

One element of kindness and culture is respect for different cultures, ethnicities, and backgrounds. We can build kindness in a multicultural context by encouraging respectful curiosity. Learning about beliefs, traditions, or practices from other places or ethnicities can create an atmosphere of understanding and respect for differences.

Regarding skin color differences, the book *All the Colors We Are* explains the biology behind skin color and can help bring student questions into very specific and less judgmental discussions. In their book *NurtureShock* Po Bronson and Ashley Merryman discuss research that indicates that it doesn't work to raise children to be "colorblind" as if color and racial differences don't exist. Rather, they benefit from the opportunity to talk about what they notice and put their thoughts into cultural and ethical context.

Sometimes kindness demands confronting racism and prejudice, which even young children may express. They've learned to be unkind about different skin colors or nationalities, and we need to confront these attitudes directly, laying down rules for language and opinions in how we refer to others. Sometimes kindness means establishing clear parameters, and a broad definition of culture is one place where that's appropriate.

 # Language

Teach children the words "please," "hello," "goodbye" and "thank you" in several different languages, making certain to include languages that are part of the heritage of children in the room.

 # World Kindness Day

Celebrate World Kindness Day on November 13. Research what others are doing and add your own ideas to the list. Spread the word to others about the day, and make it a celebration, preferably with cookies.

 # Book

Read *All the Colors We Are* and make a list of colors that people might be, including hair color, eye shadow, tattoos, or fingernails. Have children draw a number of figures with different combinations of color. Encourage them to go beyond simply calling someone's skin color "red" or "black." Notice different shades and hues that expand perspectives on color. Explore a magazine with color photos and notice the skin colors represented. Other books that address this topic include *The Sandwich Shop*, *Voices in the Park*, and *Willy the Wimp*.

Circle and Mirror

Have all your kids lie on the floor on their stomachs facing the center. Join them, creating a large circle. Have everyone put one hand in the center of the circle. Notice the different colors, shapes, and textures of each hand—how some are similar but no two are exactly alike. Notice how each color is perfect for each person just like the color of their eyes or hair, or the shape of their nose and smile.

Now ask them one by one to stand in front of the mirror and tell the class something they love about themself. Some children may need encouragement or prompting, but inevitably kids will ask to do this activity again.

Sign Language

Children love to learn sign language. Without trying to formally teach it as a language, many teachers incorporate signs into activities, games, songs, and stories. The Internet offers resources, including video dictionaries, where teachers can gather ideas and words to use.

Compassion Games.

Compassion Games offer a variety of playful ways to build compassion in a group. See link at **www.StuartStotts.com/kindness-resources/**

Curiosity or Interview

Your classroom probably includes someone from a different background or country. Could they share their culture with your students? Without putting someone from a different background on the spot and making them feel uncomfortable, children can benefit from hearing about other ways of living.

You could guide an interview or sharing time with specific questions. Ask about food, houses, birthdays, or holidays. Ask how people show kindness in their culture. Ask about differences they notice between their country and the United States. Photographs can supplement this activity.

By highlighting similarities and differences children can gain a broader understanding of the world, as well as a sense of global kindness and mutual respect. I wish some of our world leaders had more of that common sense.

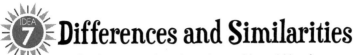

Differences and Similarities

Lead a discussion about how the world would be if everyone were the same. Ask children when they began to notice that people were different. Ask if babies notice. Ask them how people learn about differences.

REFLECTIONS•REFLECTIONS•REFLECTIONS•REFLECTIONS
REFLECTIONS•REFLECTIONS•REFLECTIONS•REFLECTIONS

Reflections for Children

1. How are people from other cultures different from ours?
2. How are they the same?
3. Why would you want to learn a different language?
4. What would it be like if you were suddenly in a different country?
5. Where did some common things in our day-to-day life like pizza, rubber, chocolate, and numbers come from?
6. What countries did your family come from originally?

Reflections for Adults

1. What do you notice about children's perceptions of difference in color, ethnicity, or culture?
2. What do you see children learning or exploring about this topic?
3. What do you notice about the influence of family on children's beliefs in this area?

CHAPTER SUMMARY

✳ **Different cultures may express kindness in different ways, but kindness is important everywhere.**

✳ **One way we express kindness is through respect and curiosity about others.**

✳ **Kindness is essential for navigating our connected and changing world.**

TOUCH

Sometimes, reaching out and taking someone's hand is the beginning of a journey. At other times, it is allowing another to take yours.

Vera Nazarian

GOALS FOR THIS CHAPTER

✳ Recognize the importance of touch in creating connections and community.

✳ Explore ways that children can safely and appropriately touch.

✳ Create specific ways to touch that build friendship.

LOU CHICQUETTE HAS worked with young children as a teacher and childcare center director for many years. He now teaches at the University of Wisconsin. Early in his career he learned about the power of touch in the classroom, and he includes touch as an essential and deliberate element any time he works with children.

During morning circle time, Lou gives kids opportunities and guidance in ways they can touch one another. Fist bumps, high fives, hugs, and handshaking are all ways to get skin-to-skin contact. He's found that starting out the day with positive touch sets a tone and atmosphere that carries through to the end of the school day.

The power of touch can help create an atmosphere of kindness. When properly introduced, touching can set the stage for defusing conflict and building bonds between children. Touch can be a great source of comfort in times of stress and sorrow. Every culture has boundaries and expectations around touch, but research tells us that the positive impact is large.

Touch can also be a tricky area for young children, because we want to be sure that they touch appropriately and can maintain control over how they touch others and how others touch them. Young children are going to hug, wrestle, poke, and pull one another. Part of a teacher's job is to guide their touching in a positive direction.

Touch may provoke difficulties in children who have been abused. It's unfortunate, but in our litigious world, teachers also must be wary of how their touching of children might be perceived.

Despite the possible challenges, touch can be a powerful force in a classroom, promoting positive social interactions and increasing children's affection and connection with one another. Furthermore, their comfort with touch will make them more likely to offer care for others in the future.

KINDNESS & SCIENCE

Dacher Keltner, a professor of psychology at the University of California, Berkeley, writes, "In recent years, a wave of studies has documented some incredible emotional and physical health benefits that come from touch. This research suggests that touch is truly fundamental to human communication, bonding, and health." Keltner adds that "Studies show that touch signals safety and trust, it soothes. It activates the body's vagus nerve, which is intimately involved with our compassion response."

Neuroscientist Edmund Ross has shown that physical touch activates the brain's orbitofrontal cortex, which is linked to feelings of reward and compassion.

Neuroscientist Paul Zak has discovered that hugs release oxytocin, a powerful molecular neurotransmitter that produces feelings of affection, trust, and generosity.

 # How to Touch

Demonstrate a variety of ways that children might touch each other to show affection: holding hands, hugging, fist bumping, putting an arm around a shoulder, shaking hands, rubbing someone's back, giving a hand to help someone get up. Make it clear that touch is always a matter of mutual consent, and that everyone has the right to maintain control over how they are touched.

 # Put Your Finger

Sing a song like Uncle Ruth's "Put Your Finger on the Finger," which moves through a variety of ways to touch: finger on finger, elbow on elbow, shoulder on shoulder.

 # Sensitivity

Increasing sensitivity to touch can build awareness. While using play dough, finger paint, sand, water, or natural shaving cream, have children pause and consider the sensations of touching, identifying characteristics like wet, hard, warm, gooey. After they wash their hands, follow up by having them touch different parts of their bodies: hair, ears, knees, etc., and describe the sensations of their own skin. If children are comfortable with one another, you might ask them to touch another child's hand in the same spirit of exploration, noticing the textures and temperatures of another person's body.

 # Secret Handshake

Have children work in pairs to create a secret handshake. Model some examples for them first. In general, limit the handshakes to three or four moves, so that they will be able to remember them. After they've created their secret handshakes, have them teach and share them with a variety of partners around the room. Make sure no one gets left out.

Knuckles or Bones

Over the last ten years we've seen the growth of people greeting each other with "knuckles," "bones," or "fist bumps." Although fist bumps can be traced back over 100 years, there's been a surge in popularity recently.

You can incorporate fist bumps into the repertoire of touch. You can also explore some of the variations like "squirrels," "DNA," and "snails." If you Google "variations on fist bump," your world will expand into new horizons of "bones."

Other Touch Greetings

In Ethiopia, men touch shoulders when they greet each other. After a handshake, Ghanaians click their fingers while saying "chale." In the Democratic Republic of the Congo, men perform a head knock in which they touch alternating sides of the forehead, like the European kiss on one cheek, then the other.

Explore these greetings with children, allowing them to carefully greet each other in a variety of ways.

Friend, oh Friend

This activity comes from Vicki Weiss, an early childhood educator in North Carolina. Although there is a melody to the song, it works equally well as a chant.

1. Children stand in front of a peer with their hands at their sides and sing, "Friend, oh Friend, how do you do? "

2. They take each other's hands, singing, "Both my hands I give to you."

3. Children turn around in a circle twice, holding hands together, singing, "Round we go and round again" twice.

4. Each child finds another friend, standing in front of a different partner, and the song repeats with the same actions.

5. Repeat as long as you or the children want. Be sure that children choose different friends each time and that no one is left out.

Reflections for Children

1. What kinds of things did you like to touch or not touch during the sensitivity activity? Did everyone like the same things?

2. If you are sad, is it helpful if someone touches you? How?

3. How did you feel when you shared your secret handshake?

4. Is it important to decide for yourself who touches you, and how? Why?

Reflections for Adults

1. What did you notice about children as they engaged in the activities?

2. What kind of rules do you currently have about children touching one another?

3. How much do you need to intervene with children during any of these touch activities?

4. What would you tell parents about today's activities?

5. What are three things you think kids need to learn about touch?

CHAPTER SUMMARY

✳ If we want children to act kindly, it helps to include healthy touch in their repertoire of expressions.

✳ Adults can help children to explore boundaries as well as the fun of touch.

✳ As in any other area, children may require adult guidance to be successful.

✳ While the benefits are great, extra vigilance is also necessary.

MOVEMENT

We should consider every day lost in which
we have not danced at least once.

Nietszche

GOALS FOR THIS CHAPTER

* Learn movement activities for children that emphasize collaboration and self-control.

* Appreciate how movement engages children's attention.

* Learn ways for children to have fun while experiencing the elements of dance.

ERIC JOHNSON HAS taught movement and dance to children for nearly thirty years. While he teaches the elements of dance—such as energy, body, and space—his classes focus on relational aspects as well. Children need to collaborate, communicate, and respect one another to create successful dances.

Eric has led workshops for teachers all over the country, demonstrating techniques and movement strategies to implement with children. He has advice for those interested in including movement activities.

Eric knows that some teachers are hesitant about exploring movement. They often feel it's an art form best left to an expert. Teachers also worry about the potential for kids to lose control or hurt themselves or someone else. Sometimes it seems easier to just keep a lid on kids' energy.

Eric offers a few principles for teachers.

- **Don't be afraid.** Children love to move and will be enthusiastic when given the chance.

- **Establish clear signals and boundaries** from the beginning, often using the same tools for classroom management as with other subject areas. You may need to spend time at first helping children practice stopping and not interfering with others.

- **You don't have to lead the activity perfectly.** In fact, it will probably take at least three times before you feel comfortable. However, this is probably not too different from leading any other type of new lesson. Getting outside your comfort zone is by definition challenging, no matter what the activity.

- Always **begin with simple warm-ups** to get children used to moving safely and to reinforce signals and directions.

- During the lesson, **keep your eyes scanning the room** to make sure each child properly performs the direction that the class is practicing.

- Successfully moving and working collaboratively reinforce general social skills and kindness in particular. However, there are also activities that relate specifically to kindness.

Eric was kind enough to share some of the language he uses. You may find your own style of communicating, but it's a good idea to start with his time-tested and well-honed outline, including his actual words.

Warm-Ups

The warm-up is essential. Stretching helps children's bodies get ready to move, and their mind's attention becomes centered on the body and movement.

Have your students stand in a circle while you lead them through the following warm-up activities:

a. **I'm blowing in the wind, blowing in the wind, blowing in the wind.**
(sway from side to side, reaching all the way to your knees)

Whoops, I'm falling crr—ash!
(hang over with head pointing to floor)

I'm growing, I'm growing, I'm growing, I'm grown!
(unfold the spine until you are standing upright)

Do this warm-up three times.

b. **Up, and down, and**
(reach arms up and down)

Side, and side,
(arms reach to each side)

Forward and backward.
(reach arms forward and backward)

Moving

Prepare your class for moving. Say something like this. **"Before we start moving, I have to teach you how to find an empty spot. An empty spot is not by a person, a wall, or any furniture. There is space around you. I'm standing in an empty spot right now. By the time I count to three, everyone find an empty spot."**

Continue preparing children to move. **"When we're moving through the room, we use our eyes in a special way. Usually we look at people and things, but when we are moving we look for big, empty spaces. Repeat that with me, 'Big, empty spaces.' Now, we'll practice. I'm going to put on the music and I'll watch while you walk, (not run, jump, twist, or roll,) but walk into the empty spaces."** Do this with students walking, and then try other movement verbs, such as gallop, jump, crawl, etc.

Partnership

Ask your children what "partnership" is. Many students will say that it's a ship for partners, while others will give a more accurate answer. Thank each respondent and continue as follows: "Partnership happens when two (or maybe three) people work together on a project and really listen and pay attention to each other. It is a little like a ship for partners because the way they work together makes it like a ship they sail on together. Learning how to work as partners is important because hardly anybody does things all by themselves: moms and dads, families, teachers of the same grade, and workers all need to be good partners."

Practice the concept. Use questions to lead your class through discovering ways that partners can move together.

1. Make this statement: **"Raise your hand if you'd like to be my partner!"** (Choose someone and then hold his or her hand.)

2. Continue: **"Girls and boys, when we work with a partner, we could certainly just hold their hand, but that's boring. Let's try some other possibilities. I'm touching knees with my partner. Now we're touching toes! What are some other ways our bodies could be connected?"** (Students will suggest many ideas; try a couple.)

3. You may need to state up front which are appropriate and inappropriate types of suggestions.

4. Then: **"I need another partner."** (Choose a second student to work with

the first student as you step back and let them work.) **"Let's hear more ideas of ways that we could connect our bodies."**

5. Ask the other students in the class to give the partners further ideas about how their bodies can be connected. The partners can try their suggestions.

6. Have children work in pairs or triads to explore different ways of connecting.

The Artist and the Clay

Teach your kids to make a fantastic shape: **"All right, girls and boys, do something fantastic with your arms. Now do something fantastic with your legs. Now with your spine. With your head. Hold it now! This is called a fantastic shape. Let's say it: 'fantastic shape...fantastic shape.' That's it!"**

Repeat the process twice more. **"Friends, I have a signal that says, 'Please make a fantastic shape.' I snap my fingers two times. Are you ready? When I snap my fingers two times, let's all make a fantastic shape."** (Snap fingers twice) **"Let's do another** (snap, snap). **And another** (snap, snap), **and another."**

Lead your children in an exploration of making fantastic shapes (shapes which employ the spine, head, arms, and legs). Choose a child as your partner and shape their body into a fantastic shape by arranging their arms, legs, posture, and head. Have the child hold the pose, and then copy it with your own body. Try this once or twice more.

Divide the class into partners. Child A forms Child B into a shape, then copies it with her/his own body. Reverse the process: Child B turns Child A into a shape, then copies it.

Notes to the adult: Students do not have to touch each other to create the shapes; they may move the partner's body parts by using invisible puppet strings or by using their voice.

Extend this lesson: Children may also play this game by turning each other into letter and number shapes.

Mirror

Choose a child to model the activity with you. You may need to sit or kneel to make this work.

Have one person be the mirror and the other the leader. The children face one another, and as the leader moves, the mirror reflects back their movements. The goal is to be a successful mirror, not to fool the other person by going too fast.

Children can work with a partner taking turns being mirrors and leaders. The goal is to develop trust and to observe another person carefully by creating patterns of movement in unison. We can listen with our eyes.

Series

Have one person create a short series of movements, perhaps three or four. Movements might include a turn, a dip, raised arms, a stomp, or a kick.

Then have that person teach the series to the whole class. Practice the series so that everyone can do it in unison.

Popcorn

In this activity, students must observe carefully and work with the whole group to imitate popcorn. The essential skill is listening and observing others.

1. Pop some popcorn, preferably in a pot on the stove or with a hot air popper. Have students observe the sound and sequence of popcorn—how it doesn't all pop at once but creates a unique rhythm of popping, starting slowly, speeding up, and then slowing down again.

2. Explain to students that the goal of the exercise is to listen to one another and create that kind of rhythm.

3. Students will start curled up or crouching on the floor, although they should be able to see one another. Have them all pop at once, rising into a standing position with their arms and legs extended.

4. Have students return to a crouching position.

5. Narrate the action. The oil is cold, it's heating up, the kernels are getting warm.

6. Tell them that the kernels are now beginning to pop. They should watch one another so that none of them pop at the same time, but they should follow each other as closely as they can.

7. Continue until everyone has popped and is standing with arms and legs outstretched.

Kindness Shapes

1. Have children make a shape that demonstrates kindness.

2. Have children pair up and make a shape that demonstrates kindness with one another.

3. Have children begin in a neutral position and move into their shared kindness position.

4. Have each pair of children share their work with the rest of the class.

5. With each pair, take some time to notice the choices they've made with movement and shape.

REFLECTIONS·REFLECTIONS·REFLECTIONS·REFLECTIONS

Reflections for Children

1. What skills helped you to succeed at these activities? (Adults can point out the collaboration and self-control children demonstrated.)

2. Did you discover a new way to move? If so, how?

3. When have you seen other people dance? What are some styles of dance?

Reflections for Adults

1. What did you notice about children's learning and growth in their ability to move?

2. What did you need to do to prevent chaos?

3. Did exploring movement bring any difference in engagement on the children's part?

CHAPTER SUMMARY

✳ Movement offers many opportunities for children to work collaboratively and kindly.

✳ Movement can be deeply engaging to children.

✳ Introducing children to dance as an art form prepares them for a lifetime of joy and health.

MINDFULNESS

Few of us ever live in the present.
We are forever anticipating what is to
come or remembering what has gone.

Louis L'Amour

GOALS FOR THIS CHAPTER

✳ Learn about the concept of mindfulness.

✳ Appreciate connections between mindfulness and kindness.

✳ Learn simple and short activities that allow children to explore
mindfulness.

IN A PRIMARY classroom in the International School of Geneva, Denise Lew led her students in a mindfulness practice. She rang a bell and asked them to focus on noticing their breathing. The students sat quietly for two minutes until she rang the bell again.

"It was difficult at first," she said to me later. "But the kids have grown so much more focused, and I see real improvements in the way they treat each other. Plus, they enjoy doing it."

Denise continued. "Mindfulness is probably easier to teach in this setting. Parents are more open to the idea than in many schools. I sure see the benefits, and I think more teachers should try it if they can."

Mindfulness is about attention. It's about being able to decide where to put your attention, rather than being distracted by inner or outer events or thoughts. It's the practice of learning to focus and be in the present moment without judgment.

Many educators, psychologists, and researchers are exploring the power of mindfulness with children. The Center for Investigating Healthy Minds at the Waisman Center at the University of Wisconsin-Madison is one excellent source for information and ideas if you wish to learn more about mindfulness in education.

KINDNESS & SCIENCE

Research has shown that the practice of cultivating empathy through compassion meditation affects brain regions that make a person more sympathetic to other peoples' mental states. Work at the Center for Investigating Healthy Minds suggests that through mindfulness training, people can develop skills that promote happiness and compassion. "People are not just stuck at their respective set points," says Antoine Lutz, a researcher at the Center. "We can take advantage of our brain's plasticity and train it to enhance these qualities."

In a 2014 study of the Center's Kindness Curriculum, "researchers found that kids who had participated were less selfish and exhibited better social skills and greater mental flexibility than children who did not do the exercises. As an added bonus the kids who did the curriculum earned higher academic marks at the end of the year."

Mindfulness is most often taught as a practice by paying attention to breath. During the practice people are encouraged to notice thoughts and feelings as they arise and then bring attention back to the sensations of breath. Over time, practitioners learn to detach from the constantly shifting currents of thought and realize that thoughts and feelings come and go, regardless of how pressing they may seem in the moment. As Vietnamese poet and Buddhist monk Thick Nhat Hahn writes, "Feelings come and go like clouds in a windy sky. Conscious breathing is my anchor."

The practice of mindfulness has grown throughout the world over the last thirty years. Mindfulness derives from Buddhist thought, but its practice has moved beyond that religious context. Business executives, sports figures, military commanders, religious leaders from many faiths, and over twenty million other Americans practiced it in 2007, and the numbers are growing.

"Executive function" is the neurological term for how our mind chooses where to put our attention. Research continues to demonstrate the value of being able to place our attention where we choose rather than where the outside world or inner thought patterns pull it. This ability to focus and concentrate is consistently important to our success in life.

Mindfulness exercises this executive function. As we become more mindful we get better at actively deciding where to put our attention.

We always have a choice in how we respond. Eleanor Roosevelt said, "No one can make you feel inferior without your permission." You are a participant in your own emotional reactions, not a victim of them.

Why does this matter for kindness? Kindness is about choosing how to act and not simply reacting to a situation. **The more control or choice we exercise in the world, the more we can choose to be kind.** We can pay attention to the self that can forgive and be generous. We can more easily perceive a need and react with compassion.

For instance, the Dalai Lama has stated that when someone hurts us, our instinctive reaction is often to hurt back. Mindfulness helps us to pause and consider how we want to react, increasing the likelihood that we will act kindly instead.

Mindfulness also helps us be calmer, which makes a difference for kindness.

Teachers should consider that children who have been affected by trauma or abuse might find this approach particularly challenging. For children who are flooded with emotions, it's important to remember that feeling anxious or frightened is real for them and marks the place where they can begin. Mindfulness isn't about suppressing feelings, even difficult ones. It's about noticing, accepting, and letting go.

Just like adults, children cultivate mindfulness through attention and awareness, by feeling their breath, and by participating in caring acts. With regular practice, children can build skills that will help them to focus, to regulate their own emotions, and to care more deeply.

Anytime you wish to practice or teach mindfulness, a few overall considerations will help.

- It's hard to teach mindfulness if you don't practice it yourself. One study showed that just 12 minutes per day impacted the quality of decisions and attitudes people experienced.

- A quiet place and time is important. Minimizing distraction is critical, especially for beginners.

- Short amounts of time for young children work best. 2-5 minutes is plenty for starters. You will be able to judge how to adjust the timing, depending on the group.

- A comfortable posture matters. You can sit on a chair, a cushion, or the floor. You can lie down or even walk.

- Practice mindfulness as an ongoing activity, preferably at the same time of day. Morning is usually best, because attention is often at its sharpest, but it can be practiced anytime.

- Use a timer so you don't need to monitor the length of the exercise.

- Explain to and discuss with children how these activities can make a difference to them.

- With those considerations in mind, try the following activities.

Sound

1. Introduce the idea of mindful posture: still bodies, sitting upright, eyes closed.

2. Ring a bell with a sustained sound, or turn a large rainstick.

3. Tell children that they should listen to the sound you are about to make and then raise their hand when they can no longer hear any sound.

4. Make the sound again while children listen for its end.

5. When the sound has died away and all of the hands are up, ask kids to move a hand to their stomach or chest and feel their breathing.

6. You might ask them to count their breaths up to five. It may be helpful to model this for them.

7. You can remind them to stay focused by saying something like, "breathing in ... just breathing out ..."

8. As children become more practiced, their ability to focus will grow.

9. After a short time, perhaps three or four minutes, ring the bell again to signal the end.

"If You're..."

Betsy Rose has adapted the song "If You're Happy and You Know It" by adding the lines "take a breath." You can watch the video of her teaching this song.

Breath

Carla Naumburg, PhD, is a writer and social worker. She suggests that young children use something concrete to help them focus on their breath. Kids can lie on their backs with a stuffed animal on their stomachs and breathe the toy up and down.

Another option is the flower/bubble breathing method. Have children hold their hands in front of their mouths as though they are holding a flower and a bubble wand. They can inhale the scent of the flower and then blow out a bubble. (Of course, you can always get real flowers and bubbles—those are great for mindfulness—but this activity works well in a pinch.)

Children can also "blow out the candle." Have each child put their hands together and raise their index fingers in front of their mouths. As they inhale and exhale, they imagine blowing out a candle. As they repeat this action, have them focus on their breath.

Glitter, Sand, and Settling Thoughts

Carla Naumburg has a daughter who is very visual, and she uses a glitter wand or glitter jar for focusing attention. (Use plastic to keep things safe.) Carla shakes it up and then her daughter watches the glitter fall to the bottom. This activity can translate to groups of children, although you may need several glitter containers so that everyone can easily see them. Have children watch carefully until the last piece has settled. This helps children to focus and to draw connections between the way feelings, like glitter, settle over time. A snow globe can work in the same way.

Author Dawn Gluskin suggests filling the bottom of a plastic jar with a bit of sand and covering it with water. Shake the jar so that all the sand swirls around. Tell the children that each grain of sands represents a thought—happy, sad, angry, etc. The swirling grains are like all the thoughts buzzing around our heads. Put the jar down and let the sand settle. As these "thoughts" settle, the water becomes clearer. The thoughts are still there, but they are no longer so active. Explain to your children that this is like the effect of meditation on the brain.

Discuss with kids how their own experience of feelings connects to this activity.

Square Breathing

Children can use 'Square Breathing," which involves counting to four as you inhale slowly, holding for four, counting out for four as you exhale slowly, then resting for four before repeating the process. Try lengthening the counts to six or even eight. This helps to focus on the breath and slow it down. After a period of counting, just breathe regularly and focus on the breath.

Ring the Bell

Have a bell in the classroom. Ring it periodically throughout the day as a signal for everyone to stop, take three mindful breaths, and then return to what they are doing.

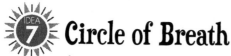 **Circle of Breath**

If your room is large enough, have your children lie on their backs in a large circle with their heads on one another's stomachs. Although they may laugh and squirm at first, let them focus on the breath rising and falling under their heads, rather than on their own. Ask them to count ten breaths of their "pillow."

REFLECTIONS·REFLECTIONS·REFLECTIONS·REFLECTIONS

Reflections for Children

1. What do you notice happens to your thinking when you sit in mindfulness practice?

2. When your mind wanders, what helps you bring your attention back to your breath?

3. Do you have any control over your feelings? Do you have any control over what you do when you feel something?

4. How do feelings change over time?

5. How does feeling calm and in charge of your attention help you to be kinder?

6. How can mindfulness make a difference at home?

Reflections for Adults

1. Does mindfulness practice make a difference in how you treat others?

2. Do you think other adults would resist the idea of encouraging children in mindfulness?

3. Which sense helps you most to be mindful—listening, smelling, touching, tasting, or seeing?

4. Does practicing mindfulness raise issues with parents and their beliefs?

CHAPTER SUMMARY

✳ There are many ways to practice the ability of focusing attention.

✳ The ability to focus has broad implications for regulating feelings and kindness, but also for other aspects of life.

✳ Children can learn and enjoy mindfulness practice.

✳ Research demonstrates that mindfulness practice helps shape our brain architecture

SONGS

Music makes you feel a feeling.
Words make you think a thought.
A song makes you feel a thought.

Yip Harburg

GOALS FOR THIS CHAPTER

✳ Learn songs that reinforce messages of kindness.

✳ Appreciate how the experience of singing together builds community and connection.

✳ Learn vocal warms-ups to facilitate group singing.

TOM PEASE IS a wonderful performer for kids, a long-term musical colleague of mine, and a dear friend. We have been in over 500 kindergarten classrooms together, working with kids to write lyrics to various songs.

Several years ago in Manitowoc, WI, Tom and I sat in kid-sized chairs surrounded by kindergarteners scattered cross-legged on a primary colored rug. The song we had chosen was called "You Gotta Be Kind." The chorus goes like this:

> **You've gotta be kind, you've gotta be kind**
> **You've got to keep your friends in mind.**
> **Don't leave anyone behind.**
> **You've gotta be kind.**

We asked kids what they knew about kindness. Within the first three responses, the word "nice" appeared, because nice is where kindness starts for young children. We kept asking, searching for specific words and images that could evoke something deeper and richer. At the end of the day, we had two verses that captured a feeling more evocative than just "nice."

> **Playground, taking turns.**
> **Playground, run and shout.**
> **Playground, in our games.**
> **No one gets left out.**

> **Friendship is a puzzle.**
> **Friendship is a dream.**
> **Friendship is a mystery.**
> **Rich as whipping cream.**

Pete Seeger said that when we sing together, we breathe in unison. Singing creates unity, not primarily through the lyrics, but through the physical experience. We sing and get connected to each other. Our defenses drop and we relax as we focus more; greater kindness is a natural result. For thousands of years, people have sung to achieve unity, and it still works in the classroom with young children.

Songs create a relaxed and connected atmosphere that facilitates learning and harmony. In early childhood, grownups sing with children for transitions, for greeting and leaving, and for cleaning up. We employ a repertoire of songs connecting to concepts like animal sounds, colors, weather, or brushing teeth. We sing for fun and to teach the alphabet. We sing because we know what an effective tool music is.

Songs also help embed ideas in our long-term memory. Significant research has shown how songs make learning stick through their connection to rhythm, repetition, rhyme, and sequencing. Early childhood teachers don't need the research to know that this is true; experience demonstrates this fact over and over.

KINDNESS & SCIENCE

Nina Kraus is a neuroscientist and professor of neurobiology at Northwestern University in Illinois. Kraus studies the effects of music on the nervous system. She says that music enters your nervous system through the brainstem, which is the foundation of knowing. "Our bodies," Dr. Kraus concludes, "are made to be moved by music and move to it."

There are many songs about kindness that can help place words and ideas into long-term rotation in kids' inner dialogue. However, I think that the real value of songs in the classroom is not about embedding or reinforcing concepts; it's about what happens to our relationships when we sing together.

One of my songs is called "Sing Your Little Heart Out Everyday." It's pretty good advice. When you sing with your children, sing with joy and gusto. Don't worry about your voice or other adults. To your kids, you are a rock star.

(Links to all of the songs mentioned are on the resources webpage.)

Warm-ups

Start your school day with simple vocal warm-ups. The purpose isn't primarily to build sophisticated musical skills, although warm-ups can teach good vocal technique. Instead, these warm-ups send a message that songs will fill the routines and activities of the day. In addition, voices will warm up, and we'll know that everyone can sing (because these exercises are foolproof.) But, before engaging in vocal warm-ups, have children turn toward each other and say in turn, "I love to hear you sing."

Warm-ups can include:

1. **The Bee.** Children make buzzing sounds, raising and lowering pitch.
2. **The Snake.** Children hiss, feeling how their breath comes from deep in their bellies.
3. **Hum.** Children hum at different pitches, moving the sound around their mouths.
4. **Siren.** Children make rising and falling pitches like a siren sound.
5. Music teachers or choir leaders can show you other vocal warm-ups.

Rainbow

Ruth Pelham's "Rainbow" connects colors and objects. It has motions that keep kids engaged. Best of all, there's a little twist at the end with the line, "The people outside my window are multicolored as can be," acknowledging diversity. The song finishes with the chorus "Rainbow around you" as everyone makes a rainbow shape around those next to them.

Sing Ruth's song, teaching motions and including children's suggestions for colors and related objects. After singing, discuss the different colors that people can be, from hair to eye to tattoo to skin to fingernails.

Each of Us Is Kind

Another of Ruth's songs, "Each Of Us Is Kind," makes the message more directly. "Each of us is kind, each of us is very smart. Each of us has lots of room/in each of our hearts/for each other as one." Sing the song with children and discuss the meaning, looking at ways that everyone can be kind.

There's value in simply repeating the understanding, like an affirmation.

 # Singing together

Sing "We All Need More Kindness in this World" with children. Sing the first verse two or three times so that children feel confident in knowing and singing. Then ask students to suggest words to replace kindness, like "hugging," "sharing," or "talking." It's fine to include silly words not directly related, but you may have to interrupt if children veer into the area of "bazookas" or "punching." Keep the focus on the positive.

 # Peace in My Fingers

Sing Susan Salidor's song "Peace in My Fingers" with children. Teach and sing the song with kids, and then make a list of other ways that hands can be kind: petting an animal, making food for someone, helping someone up when they have fallen.

Feels Good

Teach and sing "Feels Good to Help Somebody" with children. Reflect on how it feels for each of them when they help. Talk about where in their body they get this feeling. Reinforce the idea that kindness activates good feelings and that the reward is internal.

Full Sound Singing

Take any song that your students like and sing it with everyone close together in a clump—not seated around the edge of a circle—creating a full and connected sound. Sing loudly, then in a whisper, then loudly again. This activity is guaranteed to lift the spirits of all involved.

REFLECTIONS·REFLECTIONS·REFLECTIONS·REFLECTIONS

Reflections for Children

1. How does it feel to sing in a group?

2. If you were going to write a song about kindness, what words would you put in it?

3. Do you know any other songs about being kind?

Reflections for Adults

1. When you sing with your children, do you notice a difference in the quality of the relationships between you and them? Between them and other children?

2. Do you think that songs are more important for their messages or for the experience of singing them?

CHAPTER SUMMARY

✳ **Songs can reinforce messages of kindness.**

✳ **Songs can give students opportunities to add their own understandings and ideas.**

✳ **The effect of singing together reinforces a sense of community, which is central to the practice and feeling of kindness.**

STORIES

When the bond between heaven and earth breaks, only a story can mend it.

Traditional Saying

GOALS FOR THIS CHAPTER

✳ Learn basic storytelling techniques.

✳ Explore stories from several traditions that reinforce kindness.

✳ Learn ways to build upon a story's message.

✳ Recognize how sharing personal stories can build kindness.

In 1986 I attended my first storytelling performance in Santa Fe, New Mexico, where Joe Hayes enchanted a large outdoor audience with tales from Hispanic and Native American culture. I was transfixed. Who knew that simply listening to a man tell folktales would be so powerful?

Soon afterward I began to tell stories to children, and I saw the same effect sweep across their faces. They leaned toward me, silent, focused, their eyes locked onto my face. It wasn't because I told particularly well or had practiced a great deal. The power of story itself was enough.

Stories are written into our DNA and the ways we process the world. They reach a deep part of our brains. It's as if a wall comes down, and we suspend disbelief. Rationally, we know that Jack isn't climbing up a beanstalk, but in our imagination, it is as real as if we were actually witnessing his ascent. Successful politicians, preachers, teachers, and public speakers pepper their speeches, sermons, and lessons with stories. They know we will listen with relaxed yet focused attention, and their ideas will slide into our consciousness smoothly.

K I N D N E S S   &   S C I E N C E

Science writer Lisa Cron references research that shows how stories cause the brain to release dopamine, a neurotransmitter that produces good feeling and anticipation. Neuroscientist Paul Zak has shown that stories also release oxytocin, a neurotransmitter responsible for feelings of empathy and attachment. The power of story is built into brain architecture, shaped by long human history from a time when stories taught, entertained, and passed down the essence of culture.

In her book *How To Stay Sane* author Philippa Perry writes, "We are primed to use stories. Part of our survival as a species depended upon listening to the stories of our tribal elders as they shared parables and passed down their experience and the wisdom of those who went before."

It's no surprise that stories can transmit values of kindness effectively. They can lay a foundation of belief and example for a kinder life. I worry when I sense that most of the stories kids are hearing are about fighting, greed, or physical beauty. We need to offer a more balanced approach, exposing them to stories of kindness, heroism, and cooperation. And while

I'm all for reading to kids, actually hearing stories from oral traditions builds imagination, listening skills, and literacy differently from hearing stories read from a book.

Philippa Perry again. "Our stories give shape to our inchoate, disparate, fleeting impressions of everyday life. They bring together the past and the future into the present to provide us with structures for working towards our goals. They give us a sense of identity and, most importantly, serve to integrate the feelings of our right brain with the language of our left."

With basic training, any teacher or parent can learn to be an effective storyteller for young children. Using face, voice, gesture, and imagination, you can captivate children with folktales, and some of those stories can reinforce kindness.

Folktales are filled with plots in which kindness plays an essential role. A classic tale like Cinderella includes kindness to animals as a central ingredient in her eventual success. Often a main character shares his or her bread or offers assistance to someone who seems powerless or unworthy and in the end is repaid with reciprocal and often essential help. Other stories are more straightforward, promoting kindness without much nuance.

I don't like stories with morals. I believe children internalize messages more deeply when they arrive at their own conclusions and meaning. Stories offer much more than ways to transmit platitudes.

You can find resources to help you learn simple storytelling techniques in the resources section of this book. The activities included here offer a basic introduction.

 Face

Facial expression is one element of successful storytelling. Tell one of the stories from this section and then work with children's facial expressions to help them identify more deeply with the emotions.

The Lion and the Mouse.

A Lion was sleeping in the forest. A little Mouse came upon him unexpectedly. In her hurry to get away she ran across the Lion's nose. Awakened from his nap, the Lion grabbed the tiny creature with his huge paw, ready to kill her.

"Please spare me!" begged the frightened Mouse. "Let me go and some day I may do a favor for you."

The Lion laughed to think that a little Mouse could ever help him. But he was generous and not very hungry, and so he let the Mouse go free.

A few days later, while hunting in the jungle, the Lion was snared by a hunter's net. Trapped and unable to get free, he filled the jungle with his snarling and roaring. The Mouse heard the Lion's voice and ran toward him. She found the Lion struggling in the net. The mouse began to gnaw on the ropes until finally the net broke and the Lion was free.

"You laughed when I said I might do a favor for you," said the Mouse. "Now you know that even a little Mouse can help a large Lion."

After you've told (or read) the story, ask children to make faces to illustrate different emotions: sadness, anger, happiness, and fear.

Then ask students to make faces that reflect the two characters' feelings at different points in the story. You might say:

- Show me the lion's face when he has been caught in the net.
- Show me the mouse's face when the lion lets her go.
- Show me the mouse's face when the lion catches her.
- Show me the lion's face when the mouse says that she might help him someday.
- Show me the lion's face when the mouse sets him free.

Watch children's faces to assess that they are demonstrating congruent expressions.

Voice

Voice is usually the central element in storytelling. Our voices change depending on action, emotion, and character. Tone of voice often conveys more information than the words themselves.

Choose a simple word like "elevator." Say it with a number of different vocal elements: high-pitched, low, loud, soft, slow, fast. Ask children to echo you each time.

Instead of using vocal elements, use emotion. Use the same word or choose another, and have children say it expressing different emotions: sad, happy, tired, angry, scared, excited.

Reflect with them on different ways we use our voices. Choose another word and say it in a variety of ways, asking children to identify the emotion you are presenting.

The Precious Gift.

A wise woman traveling in the mountains found a diamond in a river.

The next day she met another traveler who was hungry, and the wise woman opened her pack to share her food with him. When she opened the pack, the hungry traveler saw the diamond. He asked the woman to give it to him, and she did without hesitation.

The traveler left, delighted with his good fortune. He knew the diamond was worth enough to make him rich for a lifetime.

But a few days later, he returned and gave the diamond back to the wise woman.

"I've been thinking," he said. "I know how much this diamond is worth, but I want to give it back. I hope that you can give me something even more valuable."

"What would that be?" asked the woman.

"Give me what you have inside you that caused you to give me this diamond."

What did the woman give him?

Have children say one short piece of dialogue from the story, using their voices to express the emotion the character would feel.

 # Our stories

Devote some time each week to share stories of how people were kind to you or to one other. Give kids a reason to search out kindness in their lives.

Start with a story from your own life, illustrating how you experienced kindness. Discuss your story with kids, and let them ask questions or comment freely.

Allow space for them to share as well. Make sure that the opportunity gets passed around and everyone gets a chance to tell.

Stories from the news can also play a part in this process.

Stories from Religions

Religious traditions offer stories about kindness. Although these stories might not be appropriate in secular settings, I think there's value in sharing stories from a variety of religions with children. Teachers can lead simple discussions about religion if their school environment supports respectful conversations about such topics.

The Good Samaritan

Religious stories often address kindness. This is a foundational story in Christianity and a common reference in language.

Children may need to know that Levites and priests were highly regarded in Jesus's time, and Samaritans were looked down upon.

Jesus often spent time talking with people who had questions for him. One day, a lawyer wanted to argue with Jesus. He asked, "Teacher, what must I do to live in Eternity?"

Jesus said, "What does it say in the Law? How do you understand it?"

The man replied, "The Law says that we should love the Lord our God with all our heart, with all our soul, with all our strength, and with all our mind; and love our neighbor as ourself."

"That is right," said Jesus. "Do that and you will live."

The man wanted to provoke Jesus, so he persisted. "But who is my neighbor?" he asked.

Jesus said, "A man was traveling from Jerusalem to Jericho when he was attacked by robbers. They beat him and left him lying half dead by the road.

"A priest came walking by, and when he saw the injured man, he crossed to the other side of the road, pretending not to notice.

"A Levite passed by as well. He also ignored the fallen man and crossed to the other side.

"A Samaritan was making the journey on this road. When he saw the injured man, his heart was filled with compassion. He bandaged the bleeding man's wounds and bathed them with wine and olive oil. The Samaritan lifted the hurt man onto his donkey and brought him to a nearby inn, where he cared for him.

"When the Samaritan left the next day, he gave the innkeeper two silver coins and said, 'Take care of him, and if it costs more than this, I will repay

you in full when I return.'"

Now Jesus asked the man who had questioned him. "Which person do you think was a neighbor to the man who was attacked by the robbers?"

"The one who showed kindness and mercy," said the lawyer.

"Go and do the same," said Jesus.

The Jester

This story is a Jewish folktale. We often ask children what they want to be when they grow up. This story gives a different perspective on that question.

In a faraway country, a long time ago, there was a king who ruled with wisdom and compassion. As he grew old, everyone wondered who would be the next king. Would he choose one of his children, or one of his generals or advisers?

The king wrote his successor's name in a letter, which wasn't to be opened until the day he died.

When that day came, the kingdom mourned the king's loss. After the funeral, the prime minister opened the letter and read the instructions. The king had chosen the jester.

Everyone thought this must be a mistake. How could a jester become king? But they had to obey the king's instructions. They brought the jester into the royal court and dressed him in the royal robes. They replaced his clown hat with a crown and sat him on the royal throne.

Over time the jester turned out to be a perfect choice. He was as wise and compassionate as the old king. He listened carefully to everyone, even the peasants of the kingdom, treating all with respect and kindness. He kept peace and prosperity alive in the realm. People were shocked, but the jester became a superb ruler, and everyone in the kingdom loved him.

He had a strange habit, though. Every few days he went to a room in the palace and locked himself there for a few hours. Then he returned to the throne and continued his duties. Everyone assumed he went to the room to think, meditate, or pray, and they accepted his strange habit.

One day a visitor came from far away. The visitor spent many hours with the king, gaining appreciation for his wisdom and kindness. The visitor had never known a king who listened so carefully or who asked for advice from others. He saw that this king cared deeply and worked hard for everyone's good.

The visitor also saw that the king sometimes disappeared into his distant room, and he wondered what the king did there. Was there something in that room that helped the king rule with wisdom and kindness? The visitor couldn't stop wondering.

One day when the king went to the room, the visitor secretly followed him. When the king closed the door, the visitor looked through the keyhole and watched as the king took off his crown and royal robes and put on the clothes of a jester. The king danced around like a clown, making silly faces and singing funny songs. Then he stood before a mirror and spoke to himself, pointing a finger at his reflection. "Never forget who you really are. You may look, sound, and act like a king, but you are really a jester. Never forget who you are."

Now the visitor understood the source of the king's wisdom, and that the king's kindness came from humility. The visitor loved the king more deeply and vowed to himself to keep the king's secret.

The king and the visitor became great friends. One day the visitor confessed what he had done and seen. "I promise you I won't ever reveal your secret," he said. "But I can't figure out one thing: Of everyone in the royal court, why did the king choose you? Why did he choose a jester?"

The king smiled at his friend and said, "Who do you think he was before he became the king?

The Anger Eating Monster

This traditional Buddhist story offers a solution to facing anger.

Once upon a time there was a monster that ate anger. He was never hungry. He went through the world, and every time someone argued or fought, every time there was a war or battle, the monster grew stronger and larger. He caused anger, too, by stirring up hatred or resentment, which sometimes grew into huge problems.

After a while, the monster got bored. People were too easy to anger. He thought he should try his skill out on the gods. He went to the Heaven of 33 gods, ruled by King Sakka, and seated himself at the table. When the 33 gods came in, they shouted and insulted the monster, saying, "What are you doing here, you ugly creature? You should be thrown out and cut into pieces." With every insult and angry word, the monster grew bigger and stronger. He seemed to glow with a smoky red mist.

King Sakka entered the hall and saw what was happening. He approached the monster through the mist, holding out his hand and saying, "Hello, friend. How nice of you to visit. Can I bring you something to drink or eat? Is your chair comfortable?"

With every kind word, the monster grew smaller and weaker, until he disappeared, leaving behind only a trace of stinky smoke, which soon dissolved.

Other folktales that emphasize kindness include "Beauty and the Beast," "The Bremen Town Musicians," and "Jack and His Friends."

REFLECTIONS·REFLECTIONS·REFLECTIONS·REFLECTIONS

Reflections for Children

1. How does changing your voice when you say a word with different emotions change the way you feel?

2. In the Good Samaritan story, why did the first people walk by the injured man?

3. Is it true that someone who seems weak and small could help someone who seems big or strong, like in the Lion and the Mouse? How?

4. What happens when you treat someone who's angry with kindness?

Reflections for Adults

1. What do you notice about children's attention when they are listening to stories?

2. Do you notice a difference between telling stories and reading them? If so, what?

3. Who told you stories when you were a child?

CHAPTER SUMMARY

✳ Stories are effective ways to transmit messages about kindness.

✳ Storytelling is an accessible art form that adults can learn and use.

✳ Every culture and religion has stories about the importance of kindness.

✳ Personal stories are important in building community and in understanding how kindness works in everyday life.

VISUAL ART

To draw, you must close your
eyes and sing.

Pablo Picasso

GOALS FOR THIS CHAPTER

✱ Connect visual art activities to explorations of kindness.

✱ Make kindness visible in the classroom and community.

✱ Encourage creativity, exploration, and sharing in visual art.

I AM A CASUALTY of unkind art teachers. I was told I couldn't draw well, and as a result, I don't think I can draw. It's true that I'm not skilled, but the criticism led to a lack of pleasure in visual art activities. I've gotten over that now. We should all feel open to any artistic approach, not necessarily for skill's sake, but for what we can learn, explore, and enjoy from art.

The power of unkind remarks lingers. A chance comment, an off-hand phrase can stick with children for a long time, damaging their creative confidence. Nevertheless, many kids are natural drawers and painters. Finger painting, drawing with markers or crayons, and making collages are all common activities with young children. We can use these kinds of approaches to explore kindness and enhance art experiences.

As long as they're not judging their own drawing or painting by constantly responding with, "It doesn't look like a cat" or "I wish I could draw like Toya" kids can love drawing. We want them to enjoy the process and to connect it in some way with their emotions. They don't have to name or process emotions; many adult artists have a hard time describing or even understanding what their own work is about. But they can recognize that most art begins with a feeling and expressing that feeling through art is satisfying and nurturing.

The other hope is that children will retain their sense of discovery, play, and joy at making art. Everything we do with any art form should reinforce this understanding. We don't want kids to end up feeling that if they can't draw well they shouldn't draw at all. The goal isn't to make artists, it's to keep an artist alive in everyone.

Pass no judgment on their work, but let them reflect on it with you or the group if they like, explaining why they chose a certain color or made other visual choices.

 **Abstract**

Give kids markers, crayons, or paint. Make sure their clothes are well protected. Give them several sheets of paper. Tell them to draw what happiness feels like, using just color and shape but without making realistic representations. Give them a few minutes, then try different emotions: anger, sadness, excitement, fear.

Crafts that Count

Sarah Sprague has taught young children for nearly fifteen years. She regularly comes up with craft projects for students in which they create gifts for custodial staff or neighborhood members. Projects include candles, picture frames, and paper flowers. They have also made items that can be sold to raise money for good causes.

 ## Art Show

A childcare center near Burlington, Wisconsin, has an annual art show of children's work. Often they've created pieces in the style of an artist they've studied, such as Van Gogh or Pollack. More realistic painters are not as good examples for young children. The staff matte several pieces from each child and hang them on room dividers and walls. It's very tasteful, and I've been surprised at how the work of three, four, and five-year olds takes on greater depth simply through the quality of the display. The artwork is sold, mostly to family members and friends, and the proceeds benefit a local charity. Children are very proud to show and talk about their work.

 ## Note Cards

Other centers have done something similar with notecards, using children's artwork and selling packs of four or eight cards. Many printers found on the Internet make the process of producing such cards relatively easy.

In a simpler fashion, young children can make abstract watercolor paintings that parents then cut and glue onto greeting cards to sell, raising money for a charity the kids have chosen. Previous recipients have included the Humane Society and a food bank.

 ## Collage

Collages are a time-tested activity for young children. They can practice cutting, tearing, and gluing as they gather images related to a subject. Offer children themes like kindness, helpfulness, or friendship for their collages. Once they have assembled their artwork, be sure to give them the opportunity to discuss what they have chosen and why their images reflect the theme.

Bells

Bensbells.org makes and distributes ceramic bells around Tucson (and farther) to promote kindness. With the same intention, children might make bells from metal parts or ceramics. Bells serve as a reminder of mindfulness and kindness.

Friendship Bracelets and Other Tokens

Small rocks, flowers, drawings, and time-honored friendship bracelets can help children connect visual beauty with caring. Be certain that such gifts are used inclusively.

Compassion Project

The Compassion Project is an inclusive visual art project that encourages all students to create visual images of compassion and then join them together into one piece or a large art show. Links for more information are on the webpage. www.StuartStotts.com/kindness-resources.

Kindness Chain

At Epiphany Day School in New Iberia, Louisiana, students contribute to kindness chains, made from interlocking rings of construction paper glued together, (as are sometimes seen on Christmas trees.) Every time a student sees or is the recipient of an act of kindness they tell a teacher, who then briefly describes the incident and puts the names of those involved on a strip of construction paper and glues it into a ring, adding it as a link in a chain. The chain grows longer throughout the year, functioning as a constant reminder of the presence of kindness. Children can't report on their own actions, so the whole project encourages kids to notice others.

The chains reach around the rooms, and teachers report that kindness increases, too.

Scribe

Have a child dictate to you what you should draw. You become their pencil or paintbrush. This forms a connection between the two of you, and can help kids focus on their imagination as opposed to their own skill.

 # Art Museum

Take children to an art museum. Go there first by yourself and find a few works of art to focus on. Plan for a short, focused visit. Kids like the activity, but their attention may be limited. It's also good to go over expectations for behavior in a museum before the visit.

You can explore various artistic elements like subject, line, color, or texture, and you can also find artworks that will facilitate a discussion of kindness, or lack of kindness, and its portrayal. When children recognize kindness in artworks they gain an extra dimension to their understanding.

REFLECTIONS·REFLECTIONS·REFLECTIONS·REFLECTIONS

Reflections for Children

1. What do you like about drawing?
2. What color is kindness?
3. What happens when you work with someone on making art?

Reflections for Adults

1. What is your own history with drawing or other visual art disciplines?
2. How can you encourage kids to enjoy and explore visual arts?
3. What role does kindness play in creativity?

CHAPTER SUMMARY

✳ **Everyone can enjoy making art throughout their lives.**

✳ **Art can make kindness visible.**

✳ **Gifts of art are ways for children to demonstrate kindness.**

PUPPETS

When I was a kid, I never saw a puppet show. I never played with puppets or had any interest in them.

Jim Henson

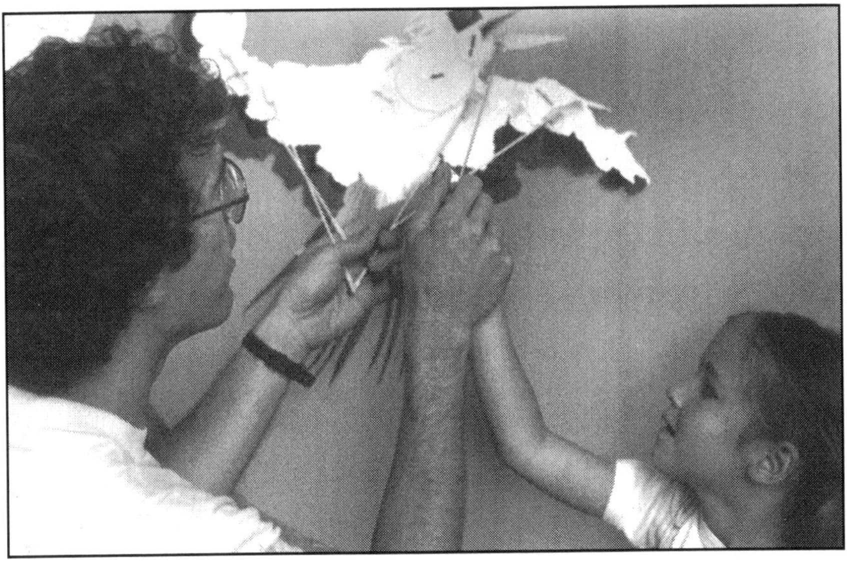

GOALS FOR THIS CHAPTER

* Learn about the power of puppetry with children.
* Appreciate how puppet play can help children explore their own understandings of kindness.
* Learn how puppets can help to address difficult or positive classroom situations.

LENORE BLANK KELNER is a teaching artist who has worked in schools leading drama activities for over thirty years. One day she checked in with a kindergarten teacher and heard that the class had been having tremendous difficulty simply coexisting. One student in particular, Joseph, had been terrorizing the class for weeks. Each week he selected one student as his target. He announced that he hated that student, and then no one in the class played with or was friendly with that child.

After an introduction and some warm-ups, Lenore took out a large square scarf. She began a drama activity called Object Transformation. She transformed the scarf into a banana and pretended to peel it and eat it. The children guessed what she was doing. Lenore then asked the students to transform the scarf into other things. Several children took turns making it into a cape, a dress, and a pillow. Lenore took back the scarf and folded it into a serpent, introducing her friend Natasha the snake to the students. Lenore began a conversation with Natasha. Natasha "whispered" in Lenore's ears several compliments about the children. Then suddenly Natasha began to "cry."

"What's the matter?" asked Lenore.

"Sneaky said he hates me and would not be my friend!" said the snake in an agonized voice.

"Why did he do that?" asked Lenore.

"I don't know but now no one in snake school will be my friend and I am so sad and lonely," moaned Natasha.

Jose interrupted. "That's what Joseph said to me, and now no one will play with me!"

The whole class was silent, stunned, to see the classroom dynamics laid bare.

Suddenly Ernesto, another boy in the class announced to Jose, "I'll be your friend."

The energy in the room was transformed. The children finished the story, solving Natasha's problem through kindness, and then acted it out. Ironically, Joseph offered many suggestions to solve Natasha's problem and then volunteered to play the role of Sneaky in the drama.

The interaction broke the cycle of bullying, at least for the time being.

Puppets are like magic with children. I consistently hear from teachers how powerfully puppets teach and focus attention. Puppets have no history with children and are impartial, and children are able to believe them.

As Lenore's story shows, puppet activities help children to embody emotions and experiences, as well as to observe interactions from a slightly more distanced perspective. Puppets allow children to process things in a "one-step-removed" manner. Children can externalize feelings or situations without talking directly about themselves. Puppets can have conversations similar to those in a classroom, and those conversations become an opportunity to notice, discuss consequences and emotions, and solve problems. Interacting with puppets can provide guidance, improvisation, kinesthetic activity, and practice for kind behavior.

As in any art form, students benefit from warm-up exercises that may not be directly connected to kindness, although they should generally encourage collaboration, self-awareness, and communication. Process and product are important. Puppet stories may emphasize kindness, but we want to be sure that children work well together, too. Learning to listen and to respect one another is central to dramatic collaboration.

Puppets don't need to be elaborate. Cloth sock puppets, googly-eyed finger puppets, and simple stick puppets can all captivate kids' attention. In fact, you may want to avoid fancy or cartoon-styled puppets so that kids can simply focus on the action and dialogue. Simple puppets are also easier for you to manipulate if you're new to the art form.

As a puppeteer, you don't need to be hidden. It's amazing how kids ignore the person at the end of the arm and just focus on the puppet.

Voices don't have to be fancy either, and a simple high and low voice can go a long way. Tone of voice is critical, though; it is such an important component of communication, and working with puppets tends to put even more emphasis on tone.

If you want to use puppets with kids, the first rule is to have fun yourself and play off of children's reactions. Build on laughter, and use that as a contrast for you to focus in on more serious moments.

Interactions

Start with hand puppets. Before presenting to kids, you may want to work with a puppet and a mirror, if only for a couple of minutes, to see how the puppets look from the children's perspective.

Have a short discussion with kids about kindness. Include words, tone of voice, and actions that demonstrate both the positive and the negative. It may be best to simply use black and white descriptors, like "kind" and "rude," so that whatever you discuss or see will fall on one side of the line or the other.

Begin by having children identify kind and unkind behaviors in puppets. Sharing a snack, using courteous words, hitting, and ignoring are actions that puppets can dramatize and that children can name as kind or unkind.

Use two puppets, one on each hand, to dramatize an interaction. Start with interactions that are kind—using manners to ask for something, picking up a dropped toy for someone else, saying "excuse me" when bumping into someone. Include other interactions that are unkind. Ask kids whether what you are dramatizing is kind or rude. Add humor and exaggeration for fun, but keep the focus on children accurately evaluating each behavior.

Opposites

After presenting straightforward interactions, use similar ones again, this time modifying the tone of voice so that it is the opposite of the perceived action. Ask, "May I please have some more cookies?" but use an angry or threatening voice. Say, "Give me those toys right now" in a kind voice. Children can identify how tone of voice is important in recognizing or demonstrating kindness. You might ask, "The puppet said, 'please' so why isn't that kind?" Kindness is at least as much about how words are said, and puppets can help to clarify this difference.

Puppet-making

Puppet making is beyond the scope of this book, but suffice it to say that kids love making puppets of all kinds. See the website for resources on making puppets. Simple stick puppets are great places to begin. The sense of ownership kids have when they've created puppets only increases their engagement.

Conversations

Puppets can ask children questions and get them to explain their understanding. Kids love to talk to puppets. They can also give puppets directions about how to act or how to respond to situations.

Stop Action

Puppets can model how to react to unkindness. Walking away from rude behavior is a good first step, and children can watch puppets do that.

Present an interaction with rude behavior and stop the action, asking children to suggest what the puppets should do in response. This allows them to explore and name strategies outside of actual day-to-day routines. Children can suggest situations for puppets to be in, and, not surprisingly, those situations will often mirror something happening in the classroom.

REFLECTIONS·REFLECTIONS·REFLECTIONS·REFLECTIONS

Reflections for Children

1. Do puppets act and feel like people?
2. What did you learn from the puppets about being kind?
3. What kind of puppet would you like to make?

Reflections for Adults

1. Why use puppets to talk about social situations or feelings?
2. How can you go from puppets to talking directly with children?

CHAPTER SUMMARY

❋ **Puppets are magical for young children.**

❋ **Puppets can help children to identify kind and unkind behaviors.**

❋ **Children can work through problematic situations using puppets as stand-ins for themselves.**

ANIMALS

People are born so that they can learn how to live a good life, like loving everybody all the time and being nice, right? Well, dogs already know how to do that, so they don't have to stay as long.

A 6-year-old boy who had lost his family's dog, Belker, to cancer.

GOALS FOR THIS CHAPTER

✳ Learn a variety of ways to help children interact with animals.

✳ Appreciate how animals can teach children about kind behavior.

SPENCER WAS A service dog and a constant fixture in the kindergarten classroom. The teacher noticed how children would often check his water dish, get him a pillow so he didn't have to sleep on the tile, or try to be quiet so as not to disturb him. "Every class should have a dog," she concluded.

Most children have an affinity for animals, if they haven't had a bad experience of being bitten or scratched. Caring for animals, holding them gently, and sharing them are all ways to reinforce kind behavior. Children often promise to love and care for their animals forever. Immanuel Kant said, "We can judge the heart of a man by his treatment of animals."

K I N D N E S S & S C I E N C E

Research has shown that as children care for animals they are more caring toward adults as well. They are also less likely to show violent and disrespectful behavior in general.

Classrooms benefit from having a pet. Such animals often become a major focus for kids. Rabbits, guinea pigs, lizards, mice, rats, hamsters, and chinchillas can make good classroom pets. In recent years allergies have grown as a concern. It seems that more and more people have allergies, and many schools don't allow animals in classrooms. If this is true for your class, it is more difficult to have real-time encounters with animals, and the ideas here may not be possible for you. Adopting endangered species animals, reading about animals, or even using stuffed animals might be partial solutions.

Oma Vic is a long-time family childcare provider. She has chickens in her back yard, and the children love to watch them, feed them, and gather their eggs. She also uses the chickens to explore treating animals well and not harassing or chasing them. Kindness is rooted in affection, and Oma Vic's kids think of these chickens as part of the household family.

Leslie Leline has worked with young children for many years in Wisconsin. She also rescues horses. The children are too young to ride alone, but they visit, pet, and sit on the horses. Leslie spares them the details of the horses' pasts, but she does give softer versions of the stories to show how they were once treated badly but are now responding well to a better life.

 # Pets

Have pets that children can care for. Talk about how to treat them and how kindness impacts their lives.

 # Gentle Touch

Animals can help children understand the idea of gentle touch. Rabbits are good for this. Supervise children in petting a rabbit, and let them feel how gentleness would feel to a rabbit. Obviously, you wouldn't allow a child to hit an animal, but you could talk about what that would feel like to the animal. You might have a child touch his or her own hand or your hand in a similar fashion to how they have touched the rabbit.

 # Animal Shelter

Arrange a visit to an animal shelter. Let children have whatever contact with animals is allowed by the rules, and talk about the kindness of those who rescue animals.

When you get back, make dog or cat treats, or measure out bags of food to give to a food pantry or to Meals on Wheels for people's pets.

 # Birds

Pinecone and other types of hand-made bird feeders have been a regular early childhood activity for years. Make connections to kindness for animals, especially in the winter. Place a feeder where kids can watch birds eating and see the results of their work.

 # Insects

Bringing bugs into the room can help kids learn to be kind to insects. Although I personally swat mosquitoes I also believe there are insects that are interesting and not harmful to people.

Kids love Madagascar cockroaches, which you can probably get from the local high school biology department. They are harmless and huge, so kids can easily see the parts of the insect. The cockroaches can crawl on the kids, and the children learn that even if a creature is "ugly" it deserves to be handled gently. This may lead to a discussion of who decides what "ugly" is. Maybe the other cockroaches think one cockroach is particularly beautiful.

Service Dog

If you know someone who has a service dog, ask him or her to bring the dog in for a visit. Discuss the kindness the dog shows to the person who needs help. Let children understand that the dog is working and isn't a pet, so that they will recognize the role of service dogs in other situations.

Chicks or Ducklings

Many children eagerly anticipate the arrival of chicks or ducks to the classroom in spring. Teachers procure the eggs from local farms or companies, and children watch the development of the baby birds. They form relationships even while the chicks are still in the shell.

Mary Siuta taught early childhood for 30 years. She says, "Though there were students I worried about, I never refused to let anyone hold or care for the ducklings, and I was never disappointed. Being kind to pets overflows to people, too."

REFLECTIONS•REFLECTIONS•REFLECTIONS•REFLECTIONS

Reflections for Children

1. What are some ways animals depend on humans?
2. Are there ways humans depend on animals?
3. Do animals deserve to be treated as kindly as people? Why, or why not?

Reflections for Adults

1. What do you notice about how children interact with animals?
2. How can you promote positive child/animal interactions?

CHAPTER SUMMARY

✶ **Animals offer opportunities for exploring kindness with children.**

✶ **Interactions with animals require careful monitoring by adults.**

✶ **Children can interact with many animals from big to small.**

THE EARTH

Now I know the secret of the making
of the best person.
It is to grow in the open air; and to eat
and sleep with the earth.

Walt Whitman

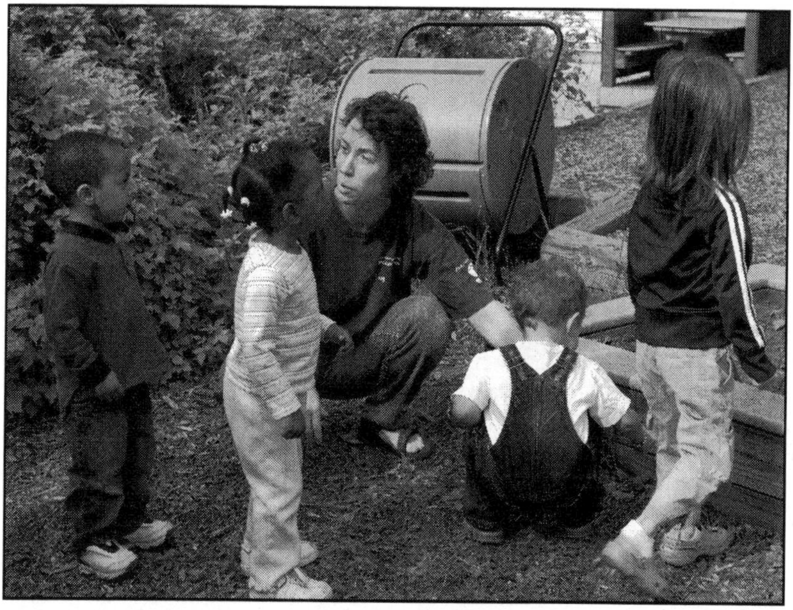

GOALS FOR THIS CHAPTER

- Recognize connections between how we treat our planet and how we treat one another.
- Learn ways to help children build understanding and relationships with the earth.
- Appreciate how wonder and beauty feed our sense of kindness.

CHILDCARE EXPERT RUTH Wilson remembers stripping bark off of a tree when she was a child. She wasn't being deliberately destructive; she was just curious and experimenting. Her father noticed and came to talk with her. He didn't scold or demand that she stop. Instead, he asked her to think about what bark's purpose is on a tree and what stripping it away might mean.

The moment made a powerful impression on her and serves as a model for how to provide guidance. Children will sometimes do things that harm plants or animals, though not necessarily out of a sense of violence. Our goal is for them to think more deeply about their actions and to bring environmental awareness into their day-to-day lives.

Bradley Miller's statement illustrates this point: "Teaching a child not to step on a caterpillar is as important to the child as it is to the caterpillar."

It may be helpful to embody our feelings about the earth and to consider treating it with the same kindness we expect from anyone we meet. Some research suggests that the way we treat the natural world reflects the way we treat one another.

Ruth Wilson calls the Earth "the birthplace of our spirit." She suggests that the "more closely we identify ourselves with the rest of life, the more quickly we will be able to discover the sources of human sensibility." Additionally, connecting children with nature helps them have more positive feelings about each other and reduces bullying.

Many years ago when I began working with students in schools, teachers often focused on environmental issues like acid rain, endangered animals, or saving the rain forest. These were worthwhile issues, but in the end they were abstract and difficult for children to connect with deeply.

KINDNESS & SCIENCE

David Sobel writes, "What happened in the childhoods of environmentalists to make them grow up with strong ecological values?" A handful of studies of this question found a striking pattern. "Most environmentalists attributed their commitment to a combination of two sources: 'many hours spent outdoors in a keenly remembered wild or semi-wild place in childhood or adolescence, and an adult who taught respect for nature.' Not one of the conservationists surveyed explained his or her dedication as a reaction against exposure to an ugly environment."

Maybe we don't need a rainforest curriculum or environmental actions. Maybe opportunities to be in the natural world with modeling by a responsible adult is the most important thing.

This is especially true for very young children. The goal is not to have them mouth slogans about pollution or whales, but to have them love our beautiful planet and act in ways that promote its long-term health.

How can young children treat the earth with kindness? Beautifying an outdoor space is one way. Being involved in household recycling is another. Sorting plastic, paper, or metal reduces trash. Planting and growing flowers or vegetables allow children to experience the earth's kindness toward humans. Many children love to cover seeds and watch them grow. Kindness flows both ways. We give and receive, and the earth is no different.

Simply experiencing the beauty of nature is another way to connect to kindness. The veins and shades of a fallen autumn leaf or the way ants carry cargo in lines can easily fascinate children. Our assumption is that knowing the earth leads to caring about it. And the earth needs all the kindness we can show it. We can't expect children to be kind to the earth if they don't know it and love it.

Connection with the earth shouldn't be reserved for Earth Week or certain days. It's a consciousness that runs throughout the year and throughout our lives.

IDEA 1 Get Outside

Let children explore the environment in their own way. Let them get dirty and take chances. There is a movement in education called "No Child Left Inside." The heart of that movement is simply that children have too little exposure to the out-of-doors. I recently read an article that talked about the calming effects of being outside, called "Nature Was My Ritalin."

A leisurely walk around the neighborhood also offers opportunities to experience and notice kindness with neighbors, animals, and each other.

Your Spot

Choose one spot outside and watch it carefully. Three feet by three feet is a good size. Return regularly to see what changes have occurred. Plants, insects, or leaves falling are examples of things to notice.

Garden

Grow a garden and teach students what it means to care for plants. The ability to care for anything over the long term, including a plant, is a way to foster the practice of kindness. If growing a garden isn't possible, growing plants in pots on the windowsill can lead kids to the same awareness.

Playground

Have children participate in keeping their playground clean. Form a line and walk across the playground, picking up any piece of litter that's in your path.

Nature Walk

There are so many permutations and possibilities for a nature walk in a park or forest preserve. Stay on the path so as not to disturb fragile plants. Experiment with listening or walking very slowly. Listening and watching are more important than biological learning.

Nests

In spring, children may enjoy leaving out nesting material for birds. Strings, bits of fabric, and strips of paper are some of the building materials for birds, and watching them gather the pieces fascinates some children.

REFLECTIONS·REFLECTIONS·REFLECTIONS·REFLECTIONS

Reflections for Children

1. Where do you like to be outdoors?

2. What's something you noticed today about nature?

3. Why do people mess up the earth?

Reflections for Adults

1. Who taught you about or simply showed you nature? Did you learn things then that you can pass on to children?

2. How can you help children cope with their fears or discomfort at being outside?

3. How can children help each other discover nature's beauty?

CHAPTER SUMMARY

✳ Kindness toward the planet is often reflected in how we treat others, and vice versa.

✳ Children need regular opportunities to experience and feel at home in the natural world.

✳ Children can experience the natural world by focusing on their senses.

HELPING

Human kindness has never weakened
the stamina or softened the fiber of a
free people. A nation does not have to
be cruel to be tough.

Franklin D. Roosevelt

GOALS FOR THIS CHAPTER

✳ Appreciate how "helping" creates positive feelings, confidence, and connections with others.

✳ Learn about essential elements of good helping experiences.

✳ Learn a variety of ways to encourage children's desire to help.

YEARS AGO I worked with a class of 2nd graders who were studying the rain forest. They were moved by the plight of animals and plants, and they set out to raise money to purchase and preserve acreage in Brazil. It was far away, but the story touched the class deeply.

Other schools raise money for other causes. They may also collect food, clothing, or gifts at holiday time. Many opportunities to demonstrate kindness through helping exist, and we can awaken children's awareness and encourage them to act.

Helping others has always been identified as a foundation and expression of kindness. Charity, paying it forward, volunteering, cooperative neighborhood efforts, and philanthropy offer avenues for people to demonstrate a desire to give to the world, and in particular, to the world beyond immediate family and friends. We help out because we can sense the bigger picture of what our world needs, and we want to participate in the process of helping or healing.

KINDNESS & SCIENCE

In his book *Give and Take* Adam Grant writes about research that explores the personal benefits to volunteering. Studies have shown positive impacts for health, awareness, happiness, and longevity for people who volunteer on a regular basis.

The research reveals three important factors for success in volunteering.

1. Long-term involvement in a cause helps volunteers get a sense of the impact of their work. In effect, people need to know that they're not wasting their time.

2. "Chunking time." Spending focused blocks of time for volunteering is better than spreading work out over several days. Volunteers are more likely to feel that they are having impact when their work is concentrated.

3. For adult volunteers, there is an optimal number of hours—100 hours a year, or two hours a week—that provides the greatest personal satisfaction and happiness.

Volunteering is most beneficial when approached with a spirit of joy and meaning. Conversely, duty and obligation don't bring out the best in a worker and don't yield the best results for the organization mission or for the volunteer's psychic well being.

Considerations for volunteer activities with young children.

1. Safety is a primary concern, whether working in a natural setting or with other people.

2. Children need to understand why what they are doing matters.

3. Children will benefit from feeling the impact of their time and effort.

4. Don't just concentrate helping activities around a holiday or certain time of year. Make helping others a central and ongoing part of routines.

 # Idea 1. Stories

Read a book or tell stories about things people have done to help others. These needn't be stories about great leaders or historical figures; instead, they can focus on small acts of helping. *A Chair For My Mother* by Vera Williams is one such book. Have kids identify things or people in their own lives that could benefit from help.

 # Cleaning Up

Identify a place outside: a small vacant lot, a roadside, or a park. Using appropriate safety measures (gloves, good footwear, awareness of traffic), work with children to clean up a given area. It may be a small area. Take a photo before and after and compare the images to demonstrate the difference cleaning up makes. Return to the place on a semi-regular basis to continue caretaking.

Raking or sweeping are good activities for children. It may help to have an adult come by and deliberately compliment kids on their work and its effects.

It's also a good idea to scope out the area first, to make sure that there's nothing dangerous or disgusting there.

 # "Jump in and Help" List

Make a list of what people in the community might need that children can provide. Some things on the list might include: picking something up, holding a door, giving up a seat, helping someone who has fallen or who is hurt.

Looking for Ways to Help

Encourage children to look for proactive ways to be helpful. While it's good to help when asked, it's even better to notice when help is needed and offer it on your own initiative.

I once heard of a job-interviewing practice. While the prospective applicant waited for the interview to begin, a worker would come through a door and "accidentally" drop a stack of papers. It was really a test to see how the applicant would react. Would they ignore the papers, offer to help, or just jump in and begin picking up? I'm not sure it was legal, but the encounter became one way to evaluate the possible new hire.

Early Childhood teacher Sarah Sprague will sometimes do something similar with her toddlers, dropping toys from a box or bag and making a game of having children help her.

Kindness is about noticing; it's an active way of viewing the world. Walking around with a perspective of "Is there something I can do here to help?" is an attitude children can learn at an early age.

Holding Doors

Holding doors open for others is a small but fundamental habit of kindness that can last a lifetime and make a genuine difference. It's not just an action to provide for people with strollers or old folks, but for anyone who is following or approaching you.

Practice by role modeling. Have one child, or a second grown-up, fill their arms with toys, bags, or boxes. Let them follow you to a door, preferably one that will close on its own. Illustrate the difference between holding the door for someone and letting them manage it on their own. Let each child try both roles, leading through the door and following through. Talk about the feelings involved in playing each role. Talk about patience. Point out that there's physical assistance that makes things easier, and also an emotional reaction that feels good or bad on both sides of the interaction.

Then practice holding doors open for people whose arms aren't full.

Children may be too small to physically manage doors in some cases, but they are not too young to practice and acquire the habit using small gates in outdoor areas or doors in playhouses.

The world would be a better place if we held doors open for one another.

Retirement Center

Visit a retirement center, lunch site, or nursing home to connect with older people. Children may want to talk about the unusual sounds, smells, and ways of relating that they encounter from older people. These kinds of visits are best done under close supervision. Helping in this case might involve drawing something for someone, listening to a story, or singing together as a group. Kindness often involves more than something physical; a song makes a fine gift, easing loneliness and lifting spirits.

Little Free Library

Little Free Libraries are enclosed boxes holding books that are free for the taking. Often placed outside in front yards, near stores, or at the entrance to schools, they offer books and ways for neighbors to connect.

Little Free Libraries are found all over the world. The motto of the movement is "Take a Book, Leave a Book." Shapes, sizes, and designs of the Little Free Libraries vary widely, but all of them are waterproof and have an easy way to access books.

Children can help to design, build, and decorate a Little Free Library and then help to maintain it, organizing the shelves, stocking new books, and monitoring titles and types available. They participate in a community service and also get a joyful focus on sharing books. You can gather books to stock the library from families, thrift stores, or library book sales.

For more information on this idea, including ideas for library designs, go to **www.littlefreelibrary.org.**

REFLECTIONS·REFLECTIONS·REFLECTIONS·REFLECTIONS

Reflections for Children

1. How does it feel to give your time to help someone else?

2. If you could volunteer to help any person or group, whom would you choose?

3. What are other ways people in the world volunteer to help?

Reflections for Adults

1. Did children find joy in their helping activities?

2. What helped them to understand that what they did mattered?

3. How will you continue to provide opportunities for children to help others?

CHAPTER SUMMARY

✳ Volunteering can bring good feelings to those who contribute.

✳ Successful helping needs a sense of purpose, accomplishment, and ongoing engagement.

✳ Starting with young children helps provide them with a foundation for a lifetime of helping.

GENEROSITY AND GRATITUDE

Piglet noticed that even though he had
a Very Small Heart, it could hold a
rather large amount of Gratitude.

A.A. Milne, Winnie-the-Pooh

GOALS FOR THIS CHAPTER

✳ Learn ways to encourage generosity in children.

✳ Appreciate that generosity is a central element of kindness.

✳ Recognize the importance of receiving gifts gracefully.

✳ Make connections between generosity and gratitude.

✳ Explore rituals and reflections to encourage gratitude.

AMANDA LANGMAN TEACHES kindergarten in Manitowoc, WI. Weather is always an issue in Wisconsin. One day during the transition from winter to spring, the snow was very wet and many of the students' socks got soaked from being outside. The next day one student brought in a bag of white socks for anyone to wear if they got wet socks again during recess.

Amanda pointed out this act of generosity, without dwelling on it. In the days that followed, she found that general helpfulness increased in her class, with students bringing in and sharing snacks and helping to clean up. One act of generosity can engender more for everyone.

Generosity is one of the finest expressions of kindness. Religions prize the ability to give and share. Generosity is recognized as a powerful virtue by anyone with an open heart. In some children, generosity comes naturally. For others it's the furthest thing from their minds. Emotions, environment, relationships, and the object to be shared all help determine the generosity a person shows and feels.

As always, role modeling is important. Any sharing that you do helps children learn. Research consistently demonstrates the importance of role modeling for anything children are learning, particularly when they are assimilating attitudes and perspectives.

Preparation can also help. Children might identify ahead of time what they want to share and what they don't want to share. As is always true when fostering kindness, focus on the good feeling inside that comes with being generous. Gandhi said, "The fragrance always remains in the hand that gives the rose." Help children to experience this fragrance.

You may need to confront lack of sharing and the conflict it creates. You can enforce equity, but you can't force generosity, although you can expose kids to the pleasures of giving and help create a habit or inclination in that direction. Children can learn to recognize generosity in others and to emulate it.

It feels good to give a gift, especially one that is well received. Receiving a gift with grace provides a gift in return.

Empathy is a powerful pathway toward encouraging generosity. When a child expresses a preference for a toy, you can acknowledge that preference and also ask the child to consider that someone else might want it, too. This helps children to recognize that others also have needs and desires.

You might praise generosity, but don't shame its absence. We should invite children to be generous and then we can notice it when we see it. We need to work out conflicts, but forcing someone to share is counterproductive. Our ultimate goal is not to create behaviors, but to reinforce the good feeling of being generous.

Gratitude is the flip side of generosity. They go hand in hand. There's a lot to be grateful for. I often hear teachers talk about the culture of entitlement that kids participate in, the sense that they deserve whatever they see or want. This sense is massively fed by the consumer culture we are all subjected to for hours on a daily basis. The fundamental message of this onslaught is that we deserve even more than the considerable gifts we already have, and that acquiring more is our God-given right. This entitlement is a recipe for disaster for each of us individually and for our planet as a whole.

Gratitude may begin with manners and with a reminder to respond with "Thank you" to gifts of any kind, but we don't want our thanks to be a hollow repetition of a well-worn phrase. We want to feel thankful and have kids experience gratitude in a genuine way.

K I N D N E S S & S C I E N C E

A 2003 study at the University of California-Davis reported that grateful people exhibit higher levels of satisfaction and happiness. Encouraging gratitude may well lead to a life-long attitude of greater joy.

Gratitude helps children look beyond their own needs and desires and prepares them for a life that will probably offer lots of disappointment. Without gratitude, even receiving good things leads to merely wanting more.

Food and Clothing

Many childcare centers or preschools gather food or clothing to share with others via food pantries or clothing banks. Children benefit from being part of this process. Have them bring in items to share.

 # Behind the Scenes

Identify someone who helps make the children's day possible, perhaps a custodian, cook, bus driver, or gardener. Make a list of what that person does and discuss what would happen if they didn't do their job. Make connections to direct impacts on the children's lives.

Write a thank-you note or letter, possibly including children's drawings, to give to that person.

 # Role-play

Practice generosity in role-playing. Explore the feelings of watching someone who has a lot from the perspective of someone who has very little. Demonstrate feelings on faces or with movement to get at the emotional impact of sharing and not sharing.

 # Receiving Gifts

Learn to receive a gift. Role-play opening a gift that you don't particularly like while still responding with gratitude and kindness. This skill can be valuable at a birthday party, where children are excited to see someone open and appreciate the gift they've brought.

 # A Thousand Unseen Hands

Look at any ordinary object or item like a chair, a glass of milk, or a shoe. Demonstrate and discuss the many hands in the chain of production that brought that item to its present place, including cooks, farmers, carpenters, loggers, transporters, sellers, and designers along the way. Reinforce with photos or pictures of the item at different stages. You might consider a different object every day.

Conclude with a sense of appreciation to the unnamed people who made the object possible.

Treats

Have a lunch or treat sharing day. Have children bring in something extra with their lunch or else bring a treat to share. Children like passing out treats. Recognizing and accounting for possibly food allergies is an act of kindness and consideration.

Penny in a Jar

"Penny in a Jar" is an activity that allows kids to contribute even small amounts of money for a cause.

Place a quart or gallon jar in a prominent location in the classroom. Use plastic, not glass. Discuss with children where they would like to contribute money. Encourage them to bring in pennies to fill the jar. While other denominations are welcome, keep the focus on pennies because everyone will be able to contribute something at that rate.

When the jar is full, celebrate and make the contribution in such a way that the children can take part. It's important that children make the choice or choices about where to give the money so that they feel a sense of connection to their work. Animal shelters, food pantries, or fundraising for someone's medical needs are often popular choices for kids.

The chorus to a related song goes:

> **Take a penny from your pocket. Put a penny in a jar.**
>
> **Kindness is like starlight; it travels far.**
>
> **Take a penny from your pocket. Put a penny in a jar.**
>
> **Kindness makes a circle back to where you are.**

Families can participate as well. Kay Phillips, a therapist, worked with a family who was by any measure below the poverty line, but who kept a jar for pennies "to give to people who are poor." There is no upper or lower limit to contributing.

Grateful "Fornaments"

You can buy glass ornaments that are open at the top and which can be filled. On small colored slips of paper have kids write things they are grateful for concerning people or things in their own lives. Fill an ornament with the papers and hang them around the room.

9 What We Have

In the book *Material World*, Peter Menzel photographed families from around the world posing in front of their homes with all of their worldly possessions arrayed around them. The stark contrast between families highlights the abundance we live with and can motivate appreciation and gratitude for the standard of living we enjoy. Even low-income households in the United States have more items than many families around the world.

Show children some of the images from the book and have them contrast what they have in their houses with what they see. The goal is not to judge but to notice the difference and encourage appreciation for what we have.

REFLECTIONS•REFLECTIONS•REFLECTIONS•REFLECTIONS

Reflections for Children

1. How does it feel to give something to someone else?

2. What would the world be like without generosity?

3. Who has shared things with you?

4. What does it feel like when someone doesn't thank you?

5. Why is it important to be grateful?

Reflections for Adults

1. What are your children's attitudes about sharing? Do they change according to time, place, item, or relationship?

2. What works well to help children share and give?

3. How do your own actions model gratitude?

CHAPTER SUMMARY

✳ Children can enjoy sharing and giving.

✳ Structured approaches and activities can increase children's ability and ease in sharing.

✳ Generosity is often dependent on many factors; it is not an all-or-nothing perspective.

✳ Exploring gratitude builds empathy and kindness.

FORGIVENESS

Forgiveness is the fragrance that the violet
sheds on the heel that has crushed it.

Mark Twain

GOALS FOR THIS CHAPTER

* Explore the importance of forgiveness.

* Learn the elements of authentic interactions around
forgiveness.

* Consider activities to build the capacity for forgiveness.

IN CHRIS'S HEADSTART class Kiera sits by her, watching the other kids play. She turns to Chris and asks, "When Devonte acts bad, do you still like him?"

Devonte has been a problem in class since the beginning of the year, and Chris has struggled to keep his behavior in line and to keep him from hurting other children. Still, Chris doesn't hesitate.

"Yes, I do," she says. "Even when I don't like how he acts, I still care about him."

Chris understands that Kiera is asking two deeper questions. One: When Devonte acts badly, should she still like him? And two: If she misbehaves, will Chris still like her?

All of us have been unkind at some point. And all of us have been hurt by others, physically or emotionally, whether it's a casual encounter with someone at a checkout counter or a prolonged emotional family relationship. Feeling hurt by others' actions is part of life, and learning to deal with that feeling, whether we are the injured or injuring party, is a powerful life lesson. Poet Alexander Pope captures this basic human condition in his famous lines, "To err is human, to forgive, divine."

When we get stuck in feeling hurt, we can't move on. We develop grudges and resentment, and that often hurts more in the long run than the initial injury. To move past hurt, we need to practice asking for and receiving forgiveness. It's a life skill that we can help children to learn. We may not always be able to allow ourselves to forgive, but we can cultivate forgiveness and have it as a goal.

KINDNESS & SCIENCE

Preliminary research confirms the deleterious physical and mental effects of not forgiving. One study found that, "Forgiveness was associated with positive emotional states as compared to unforgiveness. Granting forgiveness was associated with activations in a brain network involved in theory of mind, empathy, and the regulation of affect through cognition." In other words, forgiveness feels better.

Often, after a conflict, one child apologizes, or at least says the words, "I'm sorry" and the other child says something like, "It's okay." Sometimes the interaction is genuine, and other times kids just repeat the words that will release them from the watchful eyes of adults.

There's value even in going through the motions of apologizing and accepting apologies. Those are slightly more sophisticated forms of manners. We say, "Excuse me" when we bump into someone or, "I'm sorry" when we say something unkind, and that helps to ease the situation.

Forgiveness runs deeper than social niceties, though.

Forgiveness takes place in the emotional realm. Some describe it as an act of grace. As writer Thomas Moore says, forgiveness comes in its own time, but we create the conditions where forgiveness can occur.

Forgiveness and kindness go hand in hand. Kids can learn how to apologize sincerely, how to accept apologies, and how to let go of their own sense of guilt in order to forgive themselves.

 # First Step

When someone gets hurt, attend to the victim first. Instead of focusing on the rules that have been broken, pay attention to how someone has been injured. Keep the attention where it is needed. This can also help the offending child to focus on the impact of their actions, which is a necessary foundation for moving toward forgiveness.

 # Forgiving Yourself

Help children to let go of their own mistakes or wrongdoing. Reassure them that while you may not like what they have done, you still care about who they are.

Ask children how they feel when they know they've done something wrong. Then ask them how they have moved beyond feeling regret and sorrow.

It's also important for children to see adults admit their own mistakes. Set an example for them to follow.

IDEA 3 · Saying Sorry

Leslie Leline, a preschool teacher from Door County, WI has a specific process for teaching forgiveness and apology between young children. The steps are straightforward. Leslie stresses the importance of using someone's name and looking him or her in the eye.

1. The person who's been hurt says how they are feeling and what behavior caused the hurt. "I don't like it when you hit me with the toy truck. I was angry when you did that."

2. The person who's hurt the other says, "I'm sorry, ___" while looking into the eyes of the other person and saying their name.

3. The first person has the opportunity to say what they would like to have happen in response.

IDEA 4 · More Saying Sorry

Denise Lew, a teacher in Geneva, Switzerland, adds, "If the 'perpetrator' has acted out in frustration or anger for some reason, I often ask them, 'Would you like it if the situation was the other way around and the other person did this to you?' Usually they say, 'No', which means they are beginning to empathize with the other. However, if they are cocky or say, 'I wouldn't care,' then I become indignant and reply, 'I would care! And if someone did that to you, it wouldn't be fair and I would tell them so!' I want kids to know that I care about how they would feel if the tables were turned. At the end of the process, I never allow children to say that they promise never to do something again because something similar might happen, but instead I ask them several questions."

1. "What will you do from now on?"

2. "If you accidentally do something like this again, do you want [the other person] to come and tell me?"

3. "What would you like them to do instead?"

4. "They almost always say that they want the other to remind them that they don't like [it]. That gives them not only more responsibility, but more power to be able to speak up."

More Saying Sorry

Joellen's blog **cuppacocoa.com** offers another process. Joellen teaches and practices four steps in apology.

I'm sorry for...
This is wrong because...
In the future, I will...
Will you forgive me?

Her more detailed process follows.

1. **I'm sorry for...** Be specific in order to demonstrate to whomever you're apologizing to that you understand why they are upset.
   Wrong: *I'm sorry for being mean.*
   Right: *I'm sorry for saying everyone hates you.*

2. **This is wrong because...** If you understand why something was wrong or how it hurt someone's feelings, you are more likely to change. Showing the person you hurt that you understand how they feel is also an important part of the process of reconciliation. Sometimes, people want to feel understood more than they want an apology.
   Wrong: *This is wrong because I got in trouble.*
   Right: *This is wrong because it hurt your feelings and made you feel bad about yourself.*

3. **In the future, I will...** Using positive language, say what you WILL do, not what you won't do.
   Wrong: *In the future, I will not say that.*
   Right: *In the future, I will keep unkind words to myself.*

Have kids practice using positive language by asking them to reframe or change statements.

   Wrong: *In the future, I won't hit.*
   Right: *In the future, I will touch gently and kindly.*

   Wrong: *In the future, I won't push.*
   Right: *In the future, I will keep my hands to myself.*

   Wrong: *In the future, I won't take your toy.*
   Right: *In the future, I will ask you if I can play with your toy.*

4. **Will you forgive me?...** This is an important step to try to restore friendship. There's no rule that the other person has to forgive you. It's up to them, and sometimes they won't. Apologizing doesn't mean you automatically get forgiveness, but it's important to ask.

Role Play

You can build on the above process in role-plays. Try demonstrating an apology but omitting one of the components—for instance not saying the name or looking directly at the person. Ask for children's perceptions of emotional reactions to different ways of apologizing.

Model an interaction in which one person hurts another unintentionally and genuinely apologizes. This might include asking about the feelings of the hurt person, asking what can be done to make amends, and promising to be more careful in the future.

Ask children to imagine themselves in the place of the injured party and to recognize that person's likely feelings. Then have children imagine and name the feelings of the person who unintentionally did the hurt. Have children comment on what they observed.

Repeat the interaction, but have the person apologize without meaning it. This version might include flat facial expressions and tone of voice.

Have children comment on what they observed in each scenario, noticing when apologies seem genuine and when they don't.

Practice

Have children work in pairs to apologize to each other using the process in activity 3. Give them things to apologize for that might occur in the course of the day, but don't suggest anything too directly related to someone. Have them notice how each interaction feels in their body and what some of the clues to perceiving apologies are: tone of voice, choice of words, expressions of concern, facial expression.

Have children evaluate which interaction felt better in their bodies, no matter which role they were in.

Interrupting the Problem

It's good to have children apologize and accept responsibility. It's also important to interrupt ongoing patterns of behavior, where more than forgiveness is required. Address the problem to decrease the likelihood that it will reoccur.

Peace Table

My friends Peter and Betsy Bazur-Leidy had a table in their home designated as a peace table. We adopted the idea when my own daughters were young.

They used a blue plastic table in a corner where participants in conflict could sit and work out their problems. It wasn't a timeout spot. Sometimes adult help was required, but after a while kids could often be successful on their own. They knew when they needed to head there. There's no need to buy something special for this—simply designating a space is enough.

A similar idea can be found in the book *The Peace Rose*.

Lifeguard

Oma Vic McMurray, a childcare teacher in Madison, WI, will occasionally pull out a tall chair and ask a child to sit on it and observe other children's behavior. This may be a child who is experiencing difficulty socially. She will stand nearby, sometimes holding their hand, and watch others at play. They notice how some are playing alone while others collaborate and negotiate. Observing how others interact can serve as a learning opportunity and reveal situations where apology and forgiveness is called for.

Proactive Learning

Denise Lew also teaches a 5-finger rule that can help delineate the nature of the conflict. If someone says or does something a child doesn't like:

1. First time: Ignore it.
2. Second time: Ask the other person politely to stop. If you can explain why, that makes your case stronger.
3. Third time: Repeat your request with a stronger voice.
4. Fourth time: Repeat once more but say that if they don't stop, then you will ask the teacher to help.
5. Fifth time: Tell the teacher.

REFLECTIONS·REFLECTIONS·REFLECTIONS·REFLECTIONS

Reflections for Children

1. Why is forgiveness important? What would happen if we never forgave?

2. Is it hard to say you're sorry? If so, why?

3. What helps you to work out problems with others?

4. How can you tell when a person is truly sorry?

Reflections for Adults

1. How can you tell if a child is truly sorry?

2. Is it important to establish who's right in a conflict among children?

3. Does forgiveness fail sometimes?

CHAPTER SUMMARY

✳ **Forgiveness is an important life skill that keeps us from getting stuck in resentment.**

✳ **We can teach children ways to authentically apologize and move toward reconciliation, and we can help them to understand why it matters.**

FINALE

Be kind and compassionate to one another.

Ephesians 4:32

My daughter Cerisa and I ran a 5K race a couple of years ago. I was relatively new to running, while she had finished a marathon and a host of other races. She and I have a certain amount of competitiveness, but the truth is she was in far better shape than I was.

We trash talked each other playfully before the race began, but once we set out, Cerisa stayed with me the whole way. She could have sped ahead at any moment, but she chose to run beside me, talking and laughing, and—ultimately—encouraging me as we approached the finish line. We both finished with respectable times.

Hers was a simple act of kindness that struck me deeply. Obviously, for Cerisa, the relationship was more important than winning.

Kindness occurs in everyday actions and small moments. Kindness is not an intellectual direction, although we may consider it through an intellectual lens. It's not a learned predilection, although we may approach it through exercises and experiences. And it's not a set of perspectives, though we may nurture our awareness and practice of these perspectives in our daily lives.

Ultimately, kindness is rooted in love. We may be able to trace love's path with MRI machines, but the mystery of its power remains at the center of the healing, connection, and joy that love activates in each of us.

Love and kindness have always gone hand in hand in my life; at times they have seemed inseparable. Education classes and certification workshops don't focus on the power of love in working with children, but I believe it's what matters most. No matter what activities from this book you do, putting love at the center is what will make the largest difference.

THANKS AND ACKNOWLEDGEMENTS

I've been the recipient of so much kindness from people who shared ideas, stories, and activities in many fruitful conversations over many months. Those conversations have shaped this project. More people than I could possibly name have extended kindness to me over the years, showing me the deepest meaning of that word and attitude. To these nameless remembered and unremembered people I owe a lifetime of gratitude.

There are also people who have directly and more recently influenced my understanding of kindness and its relationship to young children, particularly in working on this book. They include, but are not limited to: Maria Arena, Pattie Ballie. Peg Barratt, Randy Barron, Rick Brooks, Cathi Burish, Sandy Byer, Lou Chicquette, Lorretta Cuff, Chris David, Richard Ely, Brigid Finucane, Charles Gamble, Eric Johnson, Lenore Blank Kelner, Amanda Langman, Leslie Leline, Denise Lew, Oma Vic Macmurray, Carol McCloud, Kevin McMullin, Ebby Melahn, Sally Meyers, Pam Mundy, Ruth Pelham, Kay Phillips, Laura Pinger, Sarah Pirtle, Ann Pleij, Deb Schein, Jeff and Mary Siuta, Daniel Sklar, Sarah Sprague, Faye Stanley, David Stokes, Lorraine Terrill, Barbara Tilsen, Michelle Watkins, Jenny Wegener, The Wisconsin Early Childhood Association and my friends there (including Mary Babula, Peggy Haack. Andrea Murray, Jeanette Paulson, and Ruth Schmidt), Ruth Wilson, and Johanna Worley.

Both of my sisters have worked with children in various ways for many years, and I'm grateful for the insights of Anna Carter and Nancy Stotts, as well as the kindness demonstrated by my parents, Jack and Virginia Stotts. And there are people who dwell in a corner of my heart, shaping my being and my thinking: Peter Berryman, Tom Pease, Charlie Knower, Barbara Chusid, Jan Ranck and Will Hayes. Cerisa, Calli, Simon, and Celeste have taught me more about kindness than I ever imagined, including how much more I have to learn. Special thanks to Calli, Cerisa, and Wojciech for their attention to the text.

And to my closest friend and compatriot in matters of heart, hearth, and heat, my wife, Heather.

Photo Credits

Hobey Ford, Will Hayes, OmaVic McMurray, Sarah Sprague, Heather Terrill Stotts, Wisconsin Early Childhood Association

Appendices and Back Pages

The following pages contain background material that may be helpful to readers wishing to consider the educational framework of this book. You will also find sources and links to further resources.

Resources by Chapter

Resources for the chapters in this book are often updated, and can be found at **www.StuartStotts.com/kindness-resources**

KINDNESS & HISTORY, COMPETITION, & TECHNOLOGY

History and Kindness

Early Christianity was marked by vitriolic debates about human nature. Are we fundamentally good, but choose to fall away from goodness? Or are we fundamentally bad and in need of redemption?

Or, as Shel Silverstein wrote more recently, "Are you good with bad habits, or bad with good habits?"

Another strand of this discussion considered whether being kind to others meant sacrifice. The authors of *On Kindness* wrote, "Kindness is not...a temptation to sacrifice ourselves but...to find solidarity with human need, and with the very paradoxical sense of powerlessness and power that human need induces."

Modern day individualists often cite Charles Darwin's theories as evidence of innate selfishness in humans. However, in the *The Descent of Man*, Darwin argued that sympathy and cooperation were essential aspects of human nature and important to evolutionary success. He believed in the importance of kindness for the survival of the human species. This wasn't a moral argument for him, but a practical one.

Many philosophers and educators have maintained that education should address the whole child, including social development. Horace Mann, a father of U.S. public education, believed that the social mission of education was to foster a richer, more compassionate humanity. School wasn't just for the three "Rs." The philosopher Martin Buber said, "Education worthy of the name is essentially education of character." Alfie Kohn, a current educational writer, interprets this to mean that, "The very profession of teaching calls on us to try to produce not merely good learners but good people."

History suggests that, whatever our belief about kindness, adults have a central role in nurturing it for children.

Kindness and Competition

What is the place of kindness in everyday life, in particular, in business and work?

Currently in Western capitalist society, the popular thinking is that someone with a "taking" or ruthless personality is more likely to come out ahead. However, there is evidence refuting this belief. In his book *Give and Take*, Adam Grant cites research suggesting that "givers" are often more successful in the long run than "takers." Focusing on giving doesn't have to mean giving up success. His book is filled with examples of how people oriented toward giving have achieved great things, and not just in humanitarian efforts.

Grant also points out that giving is not about being "nice." There are many rough-edged people who might seem harsh or abrupt on first impression but who maintain a fundamentally "giving" orientation to life.

Ultimately, he argues that a person who pursues giving and kindness is just as likely to achieve success. Even though we may see the world as a sometimes brutal place, we know that children don't need to be ruthless and callous in order to succeed.

Kindness and Technology

We don't know what the impact of the technological revolution will be on our understanding and practice of kindness. Many children spend much of their free time immersed in screens of one size or another. Does this behavior promote empathy and connection or does it dull our capacity for fellow feeling?

While there may not be a single or simple answer to that question, I do believe that young children should engage more in physical activities than in virtual ones. Many studies and medical organizations call for limits on screen time, an approach I endorse.

Young children need to interact with actual people in order to develop social skills. We can't rely on technology to teach us to be kind to one another, and we may have to compensate for children's overexposure to technological gadgetry.

In this light, one of the kindest things adults can do is to put down their phones and just pay attention to the children they are with.

HOW WE LEARN

I am always ready to learn,
Although I do not always like being taught.

Winston Churchill

While working in elementary schools I've heard too many kids say, "I hate to learn." What I believe these kids are really saying is, "I hate the way I'm being taught." Most of us can understand and relate based on our own school experiences.

Our brains are built to learn, and we feel natural internal reinforcement in acquiring new knowledge. As teachers we can profit from thinking about the process of learning, for ourselves and for our students.

Daniel Pink, in his bestselling book *Drive* suggests that three things motivate us: mastery, autonomy, and purpose (MAP for short). We like the feeling of being good at something. We like feeling self-directed, and we like being part of something larger than ourselves. He argues that external rewards, like stickers, grades, or money, work in the short term for certain kinds of endeavors, but in the long run are not only ineffective but often counterproductive. Our best learning or achieving comes from having all three elements alive in us.

The same is true for young children. Kids want to get better at things, to master skills like building with blocks or climbing a jungle gym (in centers where playground equipment is still allowed). They want to feel independent and know that their choices are valued. They want to feel part of something larger, like a classroom community engaged in a common task.

Kindness functions as a foundational orientation to life, a value, and an attitude we choose to bring to human interactions. We can help children to internalize kindness as a value that's congruent with the motivations Pink has identified, as well as using these motivations for teaching kindness itself.

Below are some of the ways people learn.

Imitation

One way we learn is by copying. We learn at first implicitly, without trying or thinking about what we're learning. No one explained walking to you, and if they had, you would have been too young to understand. You watched people walk and as you copied them, the neurons in your brain connected.

Hands-On

When we want to change how we act, or teach, or drive, we may need the words to help us outline our intentions, directions, and new information, but it's the doing that matters most. Habits, new neural patterns, and active reinforcement of acquired information bring true change. Action changes belief more than belief changes action.

Engagement

Our job as teachers is to make sure that children are engaged. If you've ever been in an average high school classroom, you've seen plenty of lack of engagement. Kids secretly text, nod off, or stare out the window. A good teacher figures out how to engage their students and how to know if they are paying attention. With young children, you can figure it out pretty quickly; they let you know when they're not with you. Key principles of engagement include:

1. working with the attention span of kids and not going on too long.

2. using a variety of teaching approaches to reach different types of learners.

3. including movement, because kids don't do well sitting still for a long time.

Repetition

Repetition is critical. As a general rule, adult learners require variety in what they learn. For children, repetition is necessary to create and reinforce the neural pathways through their as yet unconnected neural cells. This is one reason it takes a certain type of person to work with young children;

you have to be comfortable repeating actions, songs, or lessons more often than many adults would have patience for.

Multiple Modes of Instruction

Psychologist and scholar Howard Gardner introduced the theory of multiple intelligences. While the theory is still under debate and revision, there is no doubt that all of us benefit from a variety of instructional approaches through different modalities: visual, kinesthetic, and oral/aural. In traditional education, schools have placed the main emphasis on verbal learning, but we know now that students learn better when they move, sing, build, and interact, as well as listen.

Educator Bernice McCarthy developed the 4MAT system for delivering instruction. Her work is worth exploring in much greater depth, but in essence she says that students come to learning tasks with one of four questions predominant: Why? How? What? and What if? Teachers may find it helpful to make sure that they address each of these four considerations in their instruction.

The Brain is a Social Organ

The Russian psychologist Lev Vygotsky helped us find language to describe social learning and the importance of relationships and collaboration in education. We learn better when we learn and work together than when we learn separately. Most people will benefit from any kind of learning if they have someone to talk with about it and if they can problem solve or learn from other's attempts. Vygotsky insisted that social and cognitive development are intimately connected; to develop one you need to develop the other in tandem.

Cooperative learning has been a theme in education for many years. While it means different things to different educators, having children learn from and about collaboration creates opportunities for deeper learning and for kindness.

Learn it, Stretch it, Celebrate it

Vygotsky also wrote about what he called, "the zone of proximal development," which provides language for thinking about where a child is in their learning and where they can be expected to move with adult help. Every child comes to us from a different place and at a different level of development in its expression of kindness, as well as everything else. Teachers have to begin with a clear-eyed assessment of a child's developmental level before they can know what a child needs. In Vygotsky's words, "The zone of proximal development defines functions that have not matured yet, but are in a process of maturing, that will mature tomorrow, that are currently in an embryonic state; these functions could be called the buds of development, the flowers of development... that is, what is only just maturing."

We can assess what children know, stretch their learning, and then celebrate their growth.

Dynamic

Learning and teaching are fluid processes, where interaction shapes both the method and the content. Teachers may scaffold material, but learning occurs collaboratively among students and teachers rather than as the unfolding of a similar blueprint for each child. Children bring their own unique experiences, interests, and learning styles, and teachers must employ contingent strategies for individual students if learning is to become deep and meaningful.

Assessment

Teachers have to be able to assess not only where students are beginning, but also what they have learned. If students haven't understood, it doesn't matter how brilliantly a lesson was designed or what technology was employed. Assessment doesn't mean a multiple-choice test, but it does mean having a deliberate way to know what students learned and what they still need help with. Using Vygotsky's concept, we have to learn a child's zone of proximal development and how it changes as we teach and the child learns.

Purpose

Learning needs to connect to a sense of meaning or relevance. We learn much better when we can see a purpose in the material. Early childhood teachers are like hunters and gatherers, always combing the landscape looking for what will work. They have a clear purpose and little tolerance for theory and abstraction. "Can I do that with my kids tomorrow? And if so, will it make my job easier and their lives better?" The central question becomes, "Does what I'm learning make a difference to me and what I do?" If not, words and lessons don't stick.

Reflection

When we talk about what we've done or learned, we give words to the experience. A big part of early childhood development is acquiring words that help children reflect on what's happening or what they've done. Reflection brings a lesson or experience to the forefront of the brain. Activities in this book help us first to build a sense of connection and then to reflect on what we learned about kindness or anything else. We want kids to draw their own conclusions about their learning. That's the power of reflection.

If we sum things up for kids, they haven't done the work to figure it out for themselves, and they won't remember. They need to arrive at their own conclusions, even if those conclusions are not exactly what we want them to take away from a lesson. Research points to the fact that we retain information better when we've worked to get it. This is why I don't believe in sermons or morals, even if I feel good providing them. We think we've done our job if we deliver the lesson and say the content clearly, but the lesson is really only truly finished when the material has first been internalized and then verbalized through reflection.

The Arts

Another way to demonstrate and process our learning is through the arts. When we work within an art form to create a response to a subject or an experience our learning reaches deeper and remains longer. The teaching approach called "arts integration" is well suited to early childhood education, where art activities are already common classroom activities.

These learning principles run through this book, informing instruction.

1. We learn by copying. Once we know how something is done, we can do it in our own way. We adapt and innovate to fit our needs and predispositions, but we learn first by imitation.

2. Hands-on learning is best, and practice is more likely to change what you believe than belief is to change how you practice.

3. Engagement is key. If kids aren't paying attention, then we may have delivered the material but we haven't taught.

4. Kids and grown-ups need enough repetition to learn something well. Skimming the surface or grasping a concept isn't enough. We must go through a learning activity a number of times for our neural pathways to become strong.

5. We learn through different channels, so any instruction should include a variety of approaches: musical, movement-oriented, interactive, spatial, etc.

6. Learning increases when we learn together.

7. We need to know where we are starting from in terms of skills or understandings before we can move forward. In other words, it's helpful to have some sense of how much learning someone can do at any given time. We all need mastery and challenge in amounts appropriate to who we are as learners.

8. Learning is a dynamic process between teacher and student, shaped by any number of factors. There's no "one size fits all."

9. We have to be able to assess what students have learned in order to know what to teach next.

10. We learn better when what we are learning has some relevance to our experience or previous knowledge. Abstract learning without apparent purpose doesn't stick.

11. Reflecting through language helps to make our understanding explicit.

12. Arts of all kinds can help to reinforce and deepen understanding.

BRAINS AND KINDNESS 101

The way to do research is to attack the facts at the point of greatest astonishment.

Celia Green

I was presenting at an early childhood conference in 2002. One of the other presenters talked about brain research and child development. As she spoke, I felt a world open up in my understanding. I saw how structure and function were related, revealing some small piece of the infinite mysteries of the brain. The topic has fascinated me ever since, and I find over and over again that brain research supports much of what good teachers do intuitively. The importance of movement, engagement, relevance, safety, and social learning are central to what we are learning about our brains. This research also has profound implications for teaching and exploring kindness. I think it's essential for anyone working with children to have a basic understanding of cognitive neuroscience.

Scientists call the brain the most complex system in the universe. Although scientists can identify the functions of different brain regions, what's important is how the parts are connected. Because neurons can connect over a hundred trillion different ways, there's no way to replicate the same wiring from one person to another.

Our brains contain over 85 billion neurons connected through more than 100,000 miles of neural pathways. Scientists have often said that there are more connections possible between nerve cells in one brain than there are atoms in the universe. However, learning doesn't hinge on the number of neurons but on the quality and quantity of connections between them. With a system so complicated and with so many structural possibilities, we can't reduce our understanding to a few simple notions like the right brain/left brain paradigm.

The brain makes up only 2 to 3% of our body weight, but it uses 20% of our energy. It works constantly, processing, sensing, and looking for patterns, rewards, connection, satisfaction, and safety, all while attempting to avoid threat.

Different brain regions play important roles. The amygdala is an emotional center that processes danger and other strong feelings, the hippocampus is a major player in memory formation, and many other parts can be generally isolated for function. But all these parts connect in ways unique to each person.

(By the way as a side note and public service announcement, the brain needs WATER. Juice and milk are fine, but make sure kids are drinking plenty of water everyday. The brain needs water like an engine needs oil.)

As evolution has proceeded, the brain hasn't been fundamentally replaced or changed. Rather it's been upgraded, with new parts added on to the initial ones. The older, lower part of the brain concerns itself mostly with warmth, movement, food, physical pleasure, and safety. Call it the primary or primitive brain, because it developed first, and it's the part we share in some sense with lizards, fish, or even slugs. It responds to the environment, often very quickly, because reflexes are located in that part of the brain.

The second area of the brain is the limbic system. It's the part we share with horses, whales, dogs, and to a lesser extent, cats. The limbic system is concerned with emotion. Dogs connect with us emotionally. Many times when someone in my family is upset, our dog Paco will come and stand nearby or lean his head on a lap. He may not know what's wrong, but he feels that something is. A lizard wouldn't do that.

The third area, the newest part, is the cerebral cortex or frontal lobe. It's capable of thinking ahead and overruling the other areas of the brain. It's the part that says, "If I spend all my pay check Friday night, I won't have anything left for the rest of the week." It can delay gratification. This part of the brain isn't very developed in young children, who don't think of consequences when they grab candy or hit their mother because she won't let them have a toy. It's the part of the brain where higher learning takes place, too: astrophysics, poetry, humor, or crossword puzzles.

Any part of the brain can assume control at any time. When someone with a knife jumps out in a dark alley, you should hope that your primary brain takes over and you either instinctively knock the knife away or run the heck out of there. You don't want to consider the relative merits of possible courses of action. You want to escape and survive.

In the same way, if you are grieving the loss of someone close to you, the emotional part of your brain gets the attention and runs the show. You need to cry and grieve. Consolation with platitudes like, "It will get better" or, "My mother is in a happier place now" doesn't really help. You just need to feel the sadness. Sometimes children just need to cry, and we don't need to try to get them to stop. They're expressing a deep human emotion like frustration or sadness. The same is true when you feel the ecstasy of being in love. You're not inclined to think about it; you just enjoy it and ride the wave.

Successful people have a strong cerebral cortex working on their behalf. In particular, the prefrontal cortex makes decisions about where to put attention. This ability of the brain is called executive function, and it's critical to develop in children. We want kids to have the ability to stop and consider a different option or point of view and to think beyond what's immediate. Some would say that impulse control is the most basic skill for children to learn.

Executive function is also critical to kindness. It's very difficult to be kind if you're just reacting to what the world gives you. The harshness the world might sling at you can provoke a temptation to respond in kind. If someone won't share, then you won't share with him or her. That's a natural reaction. But when executive function kicks in, you might reconsider your decision. Instincts have their place, but most of the time, following primal instincts doesn't work well in everyday life. When we help kids practice and exercise executive function, we increase their capacity for kindness.

Mirror neurons are a relatively recent discovery that may be central to empathy and kindness. There is considerable disagreement over their actual impact, but the possibility of their role is intriguing.

The premotor cortex is located in the frontal lobe of the brain. "Motor" in this case means movement. The premotor cortex is activated as you prepare to move, which in turn fires the neurons in the motor cortex, which fire the muscles. Before you raise your arm to drink from a glass, the premotor cortex begins by essentially signaling the intention to the motor cortex. It's like flipping the light switch, which then opens the circuit for electricity to flow to the lamp.

It turns out that there is a subset of these premotor neurons that fire when you see someone else doing an action, and these neurons are related to the neurons in your own brain that would initiate that same action. Imagine if there are a group of nerve cells responsible for raising your arm to drink. Then imagine that there are a smaller number of connected nerve cells that fire when you see someone else drink.

These are mirror neurons, and they are one basis of imitation. It's because of mirror neurons that a baby might blink when you blink, or open and close their mouth in response to your doing the same. According to this theory, we're hard-wired to learn through imitation. Mirror neurons allow us to imitate and adopt another person's point of view at a basic physical level.

In the same way that mirror neurons are attached to muscle nerves, they also appear to work with emotions and may provide the basis for empathy. Nerve cells seem to mirror emotions and help us connect to what others are feeling.

The activity of mirror neurons is one reason that role modeling is powerful. Our minds copy what we see happening in front of us, and when behaviors are repeated, we learn them and incorporate them into our own actions. The patterns get set without our even realizing and also become difficult to change later. Dr. Haim Ginnott wrote, "Children are like wet cement—whatever falls on them makes an impression."

The primatologist Frans de Waal wrote in a paper on empathy, "Imagination activates the same representations as behavior and perception." In other words, when you imagine an action, you put the brain and body through the same steps as if you were actually doing it—though with less intensity. If de Waal is correct, then imagining an emotional connection will activate the same brain systems as if the other person were physically present.

Brain chemistry plays a role in how we experience kindness. Oxytocin is a neurotransmitter linked to feelings of intimacy, warmth, and connection. It's present between a mother and baby and is stimulated by breastfeeding.

While research in prairie voles has demonstrated the dramatic effects of introducing or withholding oxytocin, neuroscientist Paul Zak has extended its study in social bonding to our own species. He writes, "What we've shown is that oxytocin release is stimulated by acts of kindness or trust by complete strangers. The feeling people get when their brains release oxytocin is one of empathy or emotional connection."

This may account for some of the good feeling we experience from kindness. When our brains are bathed in this neurotransmitter, we feel good. In a behavioral sense, we want children to experience this feeling so they'll continue to associate feeling good with kindness and to seek that feeling out again.

What we currently know about neurology provides some understanding for how kindness works in our brains. The three-part brain, executive function, mirror neurons, and oxytocin are four lenses on neuroscience that suggest the mechanisms of kindness. Time and further research will reveal more of the specifics. For now, we can be certain that kindness doesn't just take place in the abstract ethereal essences around us, but rather in the electrical and chemical reactions in our incredible brains.

RESEARCH STUDIES

'Google' is not a synonym for 'research.'

Dan Brown

Research studies show up occasionally in this book. When dealing with research it's good to keep a few things in mind.

The ancient Egyptians believed that the heart was the center of life, and the brain was a minor player. Aristotle and, 1800 years later, Descartes, believed that the actual location of thinking was immaterial and couldn't be found in the body. Phrenology was a widely accepted belief that the shape of a person's skull was the key to understanding their personality. These ideas have proven to be inaccurate, and now we find a flood of new research changing the way we see the brain.

In the last thirty years, new imaging techniques and procedures have allowed us to peer inside at the inner workings of thought, emotion, and learning and to draw physical correlations between patterns, processes, and architecture. Not so long ago the brain was assumed to be essentially mysterious and impenetrable, beyond physical laws, functioning in its own magical universe. Some of this thinking still persists today, but we are making progress toward understanding this amazing organ.

Research and subsequent beliefs are constantly evolving. When dealing with something as complicated as the brain, we need to continue looking at data and ideas with our critical faculties intact. Research most often suggests understandings rather than definitely proving something once and for all.

Nevertheless, brain research has given us a huge gift. In general, neurological discoveries support the critical importance of early education and reinforce what most teachers know about teaching: the value of social interactions and role modeling, the power of emotion, the necessity of movement and repetition, and the need for play.

You'll find references to research studies in this book. If you are interested, I encourage you to use the references and to examine the research I note. While later research may alter our understanding, these studies represent good guesses for what we know now.

STANDARDS AND RELEVANT CURRICULUM

Instead of a national curriculum for education,
what is really needed is an individual
curriculum for every child.

Charles Handy

Much instruction in schools begins with standards. Over the last twenty or so years states have developed performance standards at all levels of K-12 education, and most have also adopted them for early childhood. Although standards address content areas like literacy or math, educators have also written standards that address social and emotional growth in young children. These standards provide a way to assess children's development, and they can point the way for further instruction.

Charles Handy's quote notwithstanding, standards provide some idea of what's to be expected and hoped for in children at various ages. Ideally we can find a balance between individualized instruction and teaching to cultural and educational expectations. Standards form one side of that scale. Whatever you may feel about standardized education, it's part of what teachers need to understand and deal with.

We can draw straightforward connections between early childhood standards and kindness, providing a rationale for focusing on emotional growth. Some parents see learning in a narrow light of literacy and math, and they may benefit from understanding that learning in young children takes place in a larger context.

While there is no national set of standards for early childhood, most states have a certain degree of consistency in areas of interest and evaluation, even if the language varies. For example, in the Wisconsin Model Early Learning Standards we find the following standards related to kindness.

A.EL. 1 Demonstrates awareness of own emotions and exhibits self-control including sample behaviors like
- waiting for one's turn
- calming oneself
- agreeing to the desires of another child

A.EL. 2 Understands and responds to others' emotions including sample behaviors like
- child identifies reasons for a friend crying
- child comforts a friend
- child recognizes another's greater need or special challenges

These kinds of standards are common in any state standards for early childhood. You can find them for your state and make relevant connections.

In addition to standards there are a number of curriculum resources that reinforce themes in this book, especially those of social and emotional growth and development. You can find links to all of these programs at **www.StuartStotts.com/kindness-resources**.

- **Second Step** features developmentally appropriate ways to teach core social-emotional skills such as empathy, emotion management, and problem solving.

- **Kindermusik** offers "ABC Music and Me." While the focus of the program is on building music competence and awareness, good tools for addressing social skills are embedded in the songs and activities.

- **Conscious Discipline**, developed by Becky Bailey, includes themes, activities, and ideas that thousands of teachers use in their work.

- **Creative Curriculum** is a resource for teachers and programs that work with young children.

- **The Center on Social and Emotional Foundations for Early Learning** offers a pyramid model for thinking about the social development of young children.

- **Responsive Classrooms** offers ways to build relationships and positive school culture.

Kindness

Before you know what kindness really is
you must lose things,
feel the future dissolve in a moment
like salt in a weakened broth.
What you held in your hand,
what you counted and carefully saved,
all this must go so you know
how desolate the landscape can be
between the regions of kindness.
How you ride and ride
thinking the bus will never stop,
the passengers eating maize and chicken
will stare out the window forever.
Before you learn the tender gravity of kindness,
you must travel where the Indian in a white poncho
lies dead by the side of the road.
You must see how this could be you,
how he too was someone
who journeyed through the night with plans
and the simple breath that kept him alive.
Before you know kindness as the deepest thing inside,
you must know sorrow as the other deepest thing.
You must wake up with sorrow.
You must speak to it till your voice
catches the thread of all sorrows
and you see the size of the cloth.
Then it is only kindness that makes sense anymore,
only kindness that ties your shoes
and sends you out into the day to mail letters and purchase bread,
only kindness that raises its head
from the crowd of the world to say
it is I you have been looking for,
and then goes with you everywhere
like a shadow or a friend.

Naomi Shihab Nye

General Resources

Books for Children

Adams, Jean Ekman. *Clarence Goes Out West and Meets a Purple Horse.* Cooper Square, 2000.

Baylor, Byrd. *The Desert is Theirs.* Aladdin, 1987.

Baylor, Byrd. *Hawk, I'm Your Brother.* Aladdin, 1982.

Browne, Anthony. *Voices in the Park.* DK Publishing, 2001

Brown, Anthony. *Willy the Champ.* Walker, 2008.

Browne, Anthony. *Willy the Wimp.* Walker, 2014.

Bunting, E. *The Secret Place.* New York: Clarion, 1996.

Graham, Bob. *How to Heal a Broken Wing.* Candlewick, 2008.

Graham, Bob. *Let's Get a Pup, Said Kate.* Candlewick, 2003.

Hoose, Hannah and Phil, Tilley, D. *Hey Little Ant.* Tricycle, 1998.

Jewell, A. *The Peace Rose.* Parent Child Press, 2006.

Joose, Barbara and Renata Liwska. *Nikolai, the Only Bear.* Philomel, 2005.

Keats, Ezra Jack. *Peter's Chair.* Puffin, 1998.

Kissinger, K. *All The Colors We Are.* Redleaf, 2002.

Marshal, James. *One Fine Day.* New York: HMH Publishing, 1982.

McCloud, Carol, illustrated by Glenn Zimmer. *Bucket Filling from A-Z: The Key to Being Happy.* Ferne Press, 2013.

McCloud, Carol , illustrated by David Messing. *Fill a Bucket: A Guide to Daily Happiness for Young Children.* Nelson, 2008.

Have You Filled a Bucket Today, Ferne Press, 2006.

McLerran, A. and Carle, E. *The Mountain that Loved a Bird.* Scholastic, 1993.

Mills, L. *The Rag Coat.* Little, Brown, 1991.

Milman, Dan. *The Secret of the Peace Warrior.* Kramer, 1991.

Minarik, E. and Sendak, M. *Little Bear.* Harper, 1978.

Muth, John. *Zen Shorts.* Scholastic, 2005.

Queen Raina of Jordan Al Abdullah. *The Sandwich Shop*. Disney-Hyperion, 2010.

Soya, K. *House of Leaves*. Philomel, 1987.

Schimmel, S. *Children of the Earth...Remember*. Cooper Square, 1997.

Van Allsburg, Chris. *The Widow's Broom*. HMH Books, 1992.

Wishinsky, Frieda and Kady Denton. *You're Mean, Lilly Jean*. Whitman, 2011.

Woodson, Jacqueline. *Each Kindness*. Nancy Paulson Books, 2012.

Books on Kindness

Davidson, Richard. *The Emotional Life of Your Brain*. Plume, 2012.

Phillips, A. and Taylor, B. *On Kindness*. Picador, 2010.

Perry, Philippa. *How To Stay Sane (School of Life)*. Picador, 2012.

Grant, Adam. *Give and Take*. Viking, 2013.

Kelner, Dachner, and Marsh, John. *The Compassionate Instinct*. Norton, 2010.

Lyubomirsky, Sonja. *The How of Happiness*. Penguin, 2008.

Books and Articles on Kindness and Child Development

Bronson, Po and Ashley Merryman. *NurtureShock: New Thinking About Children*. Twelve Publishing, 2009.

Duckworth, C. "Teaching Peace: A Dialogue on the Montessori Method." Journal of Peace Education, 3(1), 39-53. 2006.

Field, Tiffany. *Touch*. Bradford, 2014.

Harris, I., & Mische, P. "On the Relationship Between Peace Education and Environmental Education." Wisconsin Institute for Peace and Conflict Studies, 2008.

Karr-Morse, Robin. *Ghosts from the Nursery: Tracing the Roots of Violence*. Atlantic, 2014.

Kellert, S. R., & Wilson, E. O. *The Biophilia Hypothesis*. Island Press, 1993.

Levin, D. E. "Building Peaceable Classroom Communities: Counteracting the Impact of Violence on Young Children." Exchange, 30(5). 57-60.

Levin, D. E. *Teaching Young Children in Violent Times: Building a Peace- able Classroom* (2nd Ed.). Cambridge, MA: Educators for Social Responsibility and National Association for the Education of Young Children, 2003.

Louv, R. *Last Child in the Woods*. Algonquin Books, 2006.

Malone, K., & Tranter, P. "Children's Environmental Learning and the Use, Design, and Management of School Grounds." Children, Youth and Environments, 13(2), 2003.

Mische, P., E. Boulding, C. Brigagao, and K. Clements (Eds.). "The Earth as Peace Teacher." Peace Culture and Society: Transnational Research and Dialogue. pp. 139-146, 1991.

Mische, P., & Harris, I. "Environmental Peacemaking, Peacekeeping, and Peacebuilding." Encyclopedia of Peace Education. New York: Columbia University, 2008.

Montessori, M. *Education and Peace* (Helen R. Lane, Trans., original work published 1949). Chicago: Henry Regnery, 1972.

Moore, R., & Wong, H. *Natural Learning: The Story of the Washington School Environmental Yard*. MIG Communications, 1997

Roffey, S. *Helping with Behavior*. Routledge, 2006.

Small, Meredith. *Our Babies Ourselves: Biology and Culture Shape the Way We Parent*. Anchor, 1999.

Swick, K. J., & Freeman, N. K. "Nurturing Peaceful Children to Create a Caring World: The Role of Families and Communities." Childhood Education, 81(1). pp. 2-8, 2004.

Wilson, E. O. *The Diversity of Life*. Cambridge: Belknap Press of Harvard University Press, 1992.

Wilson, R. A. "Nature and Young Children: A Natural Connection." Young Children, pp. 4-11, September, 1995.

Wilson, R. A. "The Earth—A "Vale of Soul Making." Early Childhood Education Journal, 23(3), 169-171. 1996.

Wilson, R. A. "Celebrating the Spirit of Each Child." Early Childhood News, pp. 14-23. 2003.

Wilson, R. A. *Nature and Young Children: Encouraging Creative Play and Learning in Natural Environments*. London: Routledge, 2008.

Sources Cited

- Bergland, C. (n.d.). The Athlete's Way. https://www.psychologytoday.com/blog/the-athletes-way

- Cerebrum. (2015, February 2). http://www.dana.org/Cerebrum/2015/Why_Inspiring_Stories_Make_Us_React__The_Neuroscience_of_Narrative/

- Coates, J. (2014, June 7). The Biology of Risk. http://www.nytimes.com/2014/06/08/opinion/sunday/the-biology-of-risk.html?_r=0

- Cuppacocoa. (2012, June 1). http://www.cuppacocoa.com/

- Currie, L. (2014, October 17). Why Teaching Kindness in Schools Is Essential to Reduce Bullying. http://www.edutopia.org/blog/teaching-kindness-essential-reduce-bullying-lisa-currie

- Dodge, K., & Bierman, K. (2014, September 1). Impact of Early Intervention of Psychopathology.

- Eckman, P. (2010). Emotional awareness : A conversation between the Dalai Lama and Paul Ekman. Spain: Karios Editorial.

- Fist Bumps: In The World Of Global Gestures, The Fist Bump Stands Alone. (2014, July 19). http://www.npr.org/sections/goatsandsoda/2014/07/19/331809186/in-the-world-of-global-gestures-the-fist-bump-stands-alone

- Flowers, L. (2014, February 1). Unleashing Empathy: How Teachers Transform Classrooms With Emotional Learning. http://www.yesmagazine.org/issues/education-uprising/raise-your-hand-if-you-know-how-it-feels

- Gluskin, D. (n.d.). Type-A Zen with Dawn Gluskin - Live your most inspired life! http://www.dawngluskin.com/

- Gottman, J., & Silver, N. (1999). The Seven Principles for Making Marriage Work. New York: Crown.

- Hamilton, D. (2011, May 30). David R Hamilton PhD | The 5 Side Effects of Kindness. http://drdavidhamilton.com/the-5-side-effects-of-kindness/

- Hanson, R. (2103). Hardwiring Happiness: The New Brain Science of Contentment, Calm, and Confidence. Harmony.

- How the Brain Heals Emotional Wounds: The Functional Neuroanatomy of Forgiveness. (2013). http://journal.frontiersin.org/article/10.3389/fnhum.2013.00839/abstract

- Jung, E., & Ostrosky, M. (n.d.). CSEFEL: Center on the Social and Emotional Foundations for Early Learning. http://csefel.vanderbilt.edu/resources/wwb/wwb12.html

- Kirschman, T. (2012, July 1). The Corner On Character: Empathy In A (Shoe) Box Guest Post. http://corneroncharacter.blogspot.com/2012/07/empathy-in-shoe-box-guest-post.html

- Keltner, D. (2009). Born to be good: The science of a meaningful life. New York: W.W. Norton.

- Kohn, A. (1993). Punished by Rewards: The Trouble with Gold Stars, Incentive Plans, A's, Praise, and Other Bribes. Boston: Houghton Mifflin.

- Limiting Screen Time Critical for Children's Academic, Emotional Development. (2015). http://www.chicagotribune.com/lifestyles/ct-children-screen-time-balancing-20140909-column.html

- Louv, R. (2013, December 1). Nature Was My Ritalin: What The New York Times Isn't Telling You About ADHD. http://www.childrenandnature.org/2013/12/16/nature-was-my-ritalin-what-the-new-york-times-isnt-telling-you-about-adhd/

- Love 2.0 Finding Happiness and Health in Moments of Connection. (n.d.). http://www.positivityresonance.com/praise.html

- Lyubomirsky, S. (2008). The How of Happiness: A Scientific Approach to Getting the Life You Want. New York: Penguin Press.

- Maslow, A. (1968). Toward a Psychology of Being (2d ed.). New York: Van Nostrand.

- McCloud, C., & Messing, D. (n.d.). Have You Filled a Bucket Today?: A Guide to Daily Happiness for Kids.

- Meditation: What You Need To Know. (n.d.). https://nccih.nih.gov/health/meditation/overview.htm

- Naumburg, Carla, PhD | "Find Out Who You Are, and Do it on Purpose." -Dolly Parton. (n.d.). http://carlanaumburg.com/

- The Neurons that Shaped Civilization. (n.d.). http://www.ted.com/talks/vs_ramachandran_the_neurons_that_shaped_civilization?language=en

- News, C. (2008, December 29). A 'winning' smile is hard-wired into brain: Study - Technology & Science - CBC News. http://www.cbc.ca/news/technology/a-winning-smile-is-hard-wired-into-brain-study-1.761706

- One in a Million | Girls on the Run. (n.d.). http://www.girlsontherun.org/

- Paley, V. (1992). You Can't Say You Can't Play. Cambridge, Mass.: Harvard University Press.

- Perry, P. (2012). How To Stay Sane. Picador.

- Phillips, A., & Taylor, B. (2009). On Kindness. New York: Farrar, Straus and Giroux.

- Psychology Today https://www.psychologytoday.com/blog/wired-success/201010/why-have-we-lost-the-need-physical-touch

- Responsive Classroom®. (n.d.). http://www.responsiveclassroom.org/

- (n.d.). http://www.cfs.purdue.edu/cff/documents/promoting_meals/spellsuccessfactsheet.pdf

- Reynolds, G. (2010, August 25). Phys Ed: Does Music Make You Exercise Harder? http://well.blogs.nytimes.com/2010/08/25/phys-ed-does-music-make-you-exercise-harder/

- Rud, A., & Beck, A. (2000, December 1). Kids and Critters in Class Together. http://www.academia.edu/3617980/Kids_and_critters_in_class_together

- Sobel, D. (1998, November 1). Beyond Ecophobia. http://www.yesmagazine.org/issues/education-for-life/803

- The Triune Brain. (n.d.). http://www.whatonearthishappening.com/part-1-the-solution/65-the-triune-brain

- Trust, Morality —and Oxytocin? (n.d.). http://www.ted.com/talks/paul_zak_trust_morality_and_oxytocin?language=en

- http://news.wisc.edu/23437

- UCLA Mindful Awareness Research Center. (n.d.). http://marc.ucla.edu/

- Wilson, R. (2009, June 1). Color Green. http://www.academia.edu/5386527/Color_green

- Zinn, J. (1994). Wherever You Go, There You Are: Mindfulness Meditation in Everyday Life. New York: Hyperion.

Made in the USA
Middletown, DE
07 February 2017